Praise for *Yours, till Heaven*

No sermon preached in the Metropolitan Tabernacle pulpit nor any lecture delivered to nascent ministers ever conveyed greater gospel consistency or more intense declaration of truth than Charles and Susie Spurgeon's marriage. We were overwhelmed by the sense of sacred intimacy Ray Rhodes achieves in *Yours, till Heaven* by making us silent observers to the passionate lifelong love between the Prince of Preachers and his precious Susie. Their determination to keep each other in *second place*, but loving each other so much more because they made Jesus preeminent, moved and encouraged us immeasurably. This book is at times devotional, a manual, an encouragement, and a biography, but always a beautiful love story that we will never forget and that, we pray, shapes our own.

HERSHAEL AND TANYA YORK
Hershael W. York is Dean, School of Theology and Victor & Louise Lester Professor of Preaching at The Southern Baptist Theological Seminary and Pastor of Buck Run Baptist Church, Frankfort, KY

The apostle Paul teaches that a pastor's conduct at home must not be divorced from his conduct in the church or his message (1 Tim. 3:4–5). If a pastor is selfish, neglectful, and feckless in the home, it will show up in the church, and it will necessarily weaken his ability to preach with conviction. So, it is a joy to see how the godliness that Charles Spurgeon displayed in the pulpit was no ruse, but was practiced daily in his marriage. I have immense gratitude to Ray Rhodes for so adeptly demonstrating that to us in this book. There are many books that tell us how to have a good marriage. But here is something unique: a book that shows us what such a marriage looks like in the midst of all the joys, frustrations, and disappointments that life brings. Husbands and wives will do well to read this book and emulate the loving marriage of Charles and Susie Spurgeon.

JOHN MACARTHUR
Pastor-Teacher of Grace Community Church, Sun Valley, CA

An unlikely couple with strong personalities and a deep sense of humor, Charles Spurgeon and Susannah Thompson stand out for their faithfulness to each other and commitment to the Lord. In *Yours, till Heaven*, Ray's careful research and thoughtful retelling of their unlikely relationship create a marital treasure that inspires and challenges us at the same time.

STEPHEN MCCASKELL
Award-winning director, *Through the Eyes of Spurgeon, LUTHER: The Life and Legacy of the German Reformer*, and *EPIC: An Around-the-World Christian History*

Ray Rhodes takes his readers on a delightful journey into the little-known world of Charles and Susannah Spurgeon's love story. We found ourselves captivated by how they loved, and we were compelled to follow their example. Encouraging, and at points convicting, *Yours, till Heaven* is just what's needed in today's climate of self-centered approaches to love and marriage. Theirs was a love centered on Christ, a love that flowed into a joy-filled journey through both tragedy and triumph.

JEREMY AND JINGER VUOLO
Stars of the TLC series *Counting On*; host of the podcast *The Hope We Hold*

Ray Rhodes has given us a beautifully written account of the love story of Charles and Susie Spurgeon in *Yours, till Heaven*. I am truly very thankful for the deep love that my great-great grandparents shared for God and for each other, and I have learned valuable lessons from reading about their lives together. Today, I fear that marriage is losing its God-given meaning as a picture of Christ's love for His church, and people enter into this sacred union with little thought of what their marriage should look like in the day-to-day.

As you read *Yours, till Heaven* it will encourage you to love your spouse better, to support them through all the difficulties life can bring, and most importantly, to build your marriage on the sure foundation of Christ.

SUSANNAH SPURGEON COCHRANE
Great-great granddaughter of Charles and Susie Spurgeon

The beautiful love story expressed in the marriage of Charles and Susie Spurgeon offers reassurance to countless exhausted couples that deep and abiding love weathers any storm if anchored in the safe harbor of Christ. Both Charles and Susie model the diligent work of love to sustain, encourage, comfort, and strengthen one another during both the joyful and tearful times of life. Ray Rhodes serves the church well by uncovering this beautiful portrait of how a godly marriage can typify Christ when He resides at its center.

DUSTIN AND MOLLI BENGE
Dustin is provost and professor at Union School of Theology, Bridgend, South Wales

Behind the story of an extraordinarily powerful ministry is the story of a beautiful marriage written in the golden letters of kindness, forgiveness, romance, and perseverance through sorrow. Though many have heard the first story, we are in Ray Rhodes's debt for the second: the true tale of Charles and Susie Spurgeon, told realistically, grippingly, movingly, and powerfully. If you want to grow in your dedication to God and to your spouse, read this book.

JOEL (President of Puritan Reformed Theological Seminary) AND MARY BEEKE (wife of Joel, and author of *The Law of Kindness*)

As a pastor of forty-three years, I had never read a pastor's wife biography until *Susie: The Life and Legacy of Susannah Spurgeon*. Now I'm captivated by the details of a pastor and wife's deep love for one another. In *Yours, till Heaven* you will find deeper love and appreciation for your spouse and their sacrifice.

JOHNNY M. HUNT
Senior VP of Evangelism and Leadership, NAMB of SBC; former president of SBC; former pastor of thirty-three years at FBC Woodstock

When we look at the accomplishments of Charles Spurgeon, we are right to be astounded. He preached more than 600 sermons before he was 20 years of age, sold 25,000 copies of his sermons in 20 different languages every week, founded a college for pastors, authored more than 140 books, edited a magazine, responded to approximately 500 letters each week, and faithfully pastored his church in London that experienced dramatic growth. The life and ministry of Charles Spurgeon is one unbelievable story. Spurgeon was a preaching phenomenon and remains a towering figure who transcends Baptist history and impacts evangelicals far and wide. If Charles Spurgeon is the Prince of Preachers, Susie Spurgeon is his Princess. Their Christ-exalting love and affection for one another is one of the greatest encouragements of Charles's life—enabling him to labor with intensity and faithful attention to the ministry of the gospel. Ray Rhodes does an excellent job of putting on display the affection that Charles and Susie had for one another, which provides an example worthy of emulating.

JOSH BUICE
Pastor of Pray's Mill Baptist Church; founder and president of G3 Ministries and G3 Conference

When years upon years separate us from the people that live on only through their writings, it is easy for these "dead though they speaketh" types to loom large as superheroes without a single fault, and to forget they had faults like all of us. Spurgeon was one of these folks for me, which is why I thoroughly enjoyed Ray Rhodes's humble yet honest retelling of the relationship between the Prince of Preachers and the love of his life, Susannah. They were not perfect, but they were faithful. They had struggles, but they persevered. A lesson worth learning for every couple, young and old. I thoroughly enjoyed *Yours, till Heaven*, and wholeheartedly commend it to you.

MATT HENSLEE
Author of *Jonah Over Coffee*; pastor of Mayhill Baptist Church in Mayhill, NM; cohost of *Not Another Baptist* podcast

In *Yours, till Heaven*, Ray Rhodes beautifully shows how the love of Christ unites a Christian man and woman in union with one another before the Lord for life under Him. Through Ray's book, readers gain insight into Charles and Susie's love story that provides Christian couples today through their example of what an enduring Christian marriage grounded and shaped by the Word looks like, along with the effects such a marriage can have on our world today.

DAVE JENKINS
Executive Director, Servants of Grace; Executive Editor, *Theology for Life Magazine*; host, *Equipping You in Grace*, *Servants of Grace*, and *Warriors of Grace* podcasts

Yours, till Heaven

The Untold Love Story of Charles and Susie Spurgeon

RAY RHODES JR.

MOODY PUBLISHERS
CHICAGO

Edited by Amanda Cleary Eastep
Interior and cover design: Erik M. Peterson
Cover border illustration copyright © 2019 by Fourleaflover/iStock (1159833770). All rights reserved.
Cover portraits of Charles and Susannah Spurgeon courtesy of Internet Archive Book Images. Public domain.
Author photo: Rachel Rink

Library of Congress Cataloging-in-Publication Data

Names: Rhodes, Ray, Jr., author.
Title: Yours, till heaven : the untold love story of Charles and Susie
    Spurgeon / Ray Rhodes, Jr.
Description: Chicago : Moody Publishers, [2021] | Includes bibliographical
    references. | Summary: "Yours, Till Heaven invites you into the untold
    love story of Charles and Susie Spurgeon to discover how the bond
    between this renowned couple helped fuel their lifelong service to the
    Lord. Discover how Charles and Susie traversed the challenges of
    physical affliction, popularity, controversy, and other trials together
    with a heavenly vision"-- Provided by publisher.
Identifiers: LCCN 2020035557 (print) | LCCN 2020035558 (ebook) | ISBN
    9780802419521 | ISBN 9780802498151 (ebook)
Subjects: LCSH: Spurgeon, C. H. (Charles Haddon), 1834-1892. | Spurgeon,
    Susannah, -1903. | Baptists--England--Biography. |
    Evangelists--England--Biography.
Classification: LCC BX6493 .R47 2021 (print) | LCC BX6493 (ebook) | DDC
    286/.10922 [B]--dc23
LC record available at https://lccn.loc.gov/2020035557
LC ebook record available at https://lccn.loc.gov/2020035558

Originally delivered by fleets of horse-drawn wagons, the affordable paperbacks from D. L. Moody's publishing house resourced the church and served everyday people. Now, after more than 125 years of publishing and ministry, Moody Publishers' mission remains the same—even if our delivery systems have changed a bit. For more information on other books (and resources) created from a biblical perspective, go to www.moodypublishers.com or write to:

Moody Publishers
820 N. LaSalle Boulevard
Chicago, IL 60610

1 3 5 7 9 10 8 6 4 2

Printed in the United States of America

To the love of my life, Lori. One of my favorite adventures with you was our journey to England and France as we chased Charles and Susie from majestic London to idyllic Mentone with stops in various and sundry places, including romantic Paris.

Kissing you on top of the Eiffel Tower was like a "fairy dream."

Walking with you through Hanbury Gardens seemed Edenic.

Meandering through the streets of London with you, unforgettable.

Seeing Christ in you, the ultimate.

Yours, till heaven, *and then.*

Ray

Contents

Foreword

LIKE GEORGE WHITEFIELD IN THE CENTURY BEFORE and Billy Graham in the century after, Charles Spurgeon's ministry enjoyed an unrivaled influence in the nineteenth century. Spurgeon stepped onto the global Christian stage barely into his adulthood and walked across it for the next four decades. The obvious fact that God's hand rested on his life and ministry gives Spurgeon a certain mystique to this day.

By most every measure, Spurgeon was a phenom. His mind was electric, his energy indefatigable, his ministerial reach global, his courage unbendable, his calling sure and steady. All of this and more enabled Spurgeon to accomplish remarkable feat after remarkable feat.

In a sense, all of his ministerial influence flowed from his pulpit ministry. Yes, Spurgeon founded more than five dozen ministries and auxiliary efforts (including orphanages and a pastors' college, both of which are still in operation), but what came from his pulpit drew people to him in his life and keeps drawing people to him today.

In fact, conventional assessments of Spurgeon point to his pulpit ministry as the engine that powered his broader, ministerial influence. He was a lion in the pulpit, roaring forth God's truth sermon by sermon. His preaching was both convicting and compelling. The masses attended services out of curiosity; they often left transformed.

Spurgeon's daily mail was filled with speaking requests. He lived in great demand, often preaching ten times in a single week. Once, he preached to an audience of 23,654 without a microphone or modern means of amplification. What is more, during his lifetime, Spurgeon preached to an estimated ten million people.

In his lifetime, Charles Spurgeon's sermons were transcribed, edited, and distributed around the globe. In total, Spurgeon is history's most widely read preacher. To this day, we have available more material written by Spurgeon than by any other Christian author. For instance, Spurgeon's collected sermons, as published in *The New Park Street Pulpit* and *The Metropolitan Tabernacle Pulpit*, fill sixty-three volumes.

Spurgeon, however, pointed not to his pulpit ministry but to the Holy Spirit as the genesis of his success. He often worked eighteen hours a day, months on end. When the famous missionary-explorer David Livingstone inquired of Spurgeon how he did the work of two men, Spurgeon, referring to the Holy Spirit, said, "You have forgotten that there are two of us." Indeed, Spurgeon was not only gifted by the Holy Spirit, but also empowered by Him.

Yet there's an even more intimate, personal side of Spurgeon that enabled God to use him so. Just as Joshua and Aaron held up Moses's arms in Exodus 17, thus enabling victory in battle, so Susie Spurgeon held up her beloved's arms, year after year, decade after decade. In so doing, she extended not only the reach of her husband's ministry, but also the duration of it.

Yet their marriage should not be thought of as a business arrangement. Their marriage knew romance, love, and mutual affection. This affection prompted mutual support and sacrifice.

Unpacking the Spurgeons' love story is the genius of Ray Rhodes's work. Like his previous book, *Susie: The Life and Legacy of*

Susannah Spurgeon, Wife of Charles H. Spurgeon, Rhodes's *Yours, till Heaven* gives us an intimate look at the personal lives of Charles and Susie Spurgeon, and in so doing, inspires a new generation of ministry couples.

Those who are intrigued by Spurgeon will find this volume of interest, from start to finish. Rhodes marshals previously overlooked facts and underwritten upon aspects of Spurgeon's life, marriage, and ministry.

More broadly, every minister and ministry spouse will doubtlessly find both instruction and encouragement as they read this fresh examination of Charles and Susie Spurgeon's love story.

The challenges of ministry are best endured with a spouse who walks with us. The blessings of ministry are made sweeter by the same. Read *Yours, till Heaven* and be better prepared for both.

JASON K. ALLEN
President, Midwestern Baptist Theological Seminary

Timeline

JANUARY 15, 1832:
Susie is born to R. B. and Susannah Thompson
in London, England.

JUNE 19, 1834:
Charles Haddon Spurgeon is born to John and Eliza Spurgeon
in Kelvedon.

1837–1901:
The Reign of Queen Victoria

JANUARY 6, 1850:
Charles Spurgeon is converted at the Primitive Methodist Chapel
in Colchester.

MAY 3, 1850:
Charles is baptized in the River Lark at Isleham Ferry.

OCTOBER 3, 1850:
Charles joins the St. Andrew's Street Baptist Church
in Cambridge.

OCTOBER, 1851:
Charles becomes pastor of Waterbeach Baptist Chapel.

WINTER, 1852:
Susie Thompson is converted at the Poultry Chapel in London.

DECEMBER 18, 1853:

Charles preaches at the New Park Street Chapel (NPSC).

APRIL 20, 1854:

Charles gives Susie Thompson a copy of *The Pilgrim's Progress*.

APRIL 28, 1854:

Charles is formally installed as pastor of NPSC.

JUNE 10, 1854:

Charles reveals his feelings for Susie
at the grand reopening of the Crystal Palace.

AUGUST 2, 1854:

Charles and Susie are engaged.

FEBRUARY 1, 1855:

Charles baptizes Susie at NPSC.

JANUARY 8, 1856:

Charles and Susie are married at a morning wedding at NPSC.

SEPTEMBER 20, 1856:

Susie gives birth to twin sons, Charles and Thomas.

OCTOBER 19, 1856:

Surrey Gardens Music Hall disaster.

MARCH 18, 1861:

The Metropolitan Tabernacle opens.

1866:

Charles starts the monthly publication, *The Sword and the Trowel*.

LATE 1868:

Dr. James Simpson performs surgery on Susie
for a gynecological issue.

1875:

Thomas Johnson begins his studies at the Pastors' College.
Charles releases volume one of *Lectures to My Students*.
Susie Spurgeon's Book Fund begins.

1880:

Charles and Susie move to their final home, Westwood,
near the Crystal Palace.

1887–1889:

The Down-Grade Controversy.

1889:

Susie joins Beulah Baptist Church, Thornton Heath,
near Westwood (she also remains a member
of the Metropolitan Tabernacle).

JANUARY 31, 1892:

Charles dies at the Hôtel Beau Rivage in Mentone, France.
Susie is with him.

FEBRUARY 11, 1892:

Charles is buried at the West Norwood Cemetery,
near Westwood.

1897–1900:

Susie co-edits and significantly contributes
to *C. H. Spurgeon's Autobiography*.

OCTOBER 22, 1903:

Susie dies at her home, Westwood.

OCTOBER 27, 1903:

Susie's funeral is held at Chatsworth Road Baptist Chapel.
She is entombed with Charles at the West Norwood Cemetery.

How to Read This Book

YOURS, TILL HEAVEN IS THE LOVE STORY of Charles and Susie Spurgeon from a thematic rather than a purely chronological perspective. Though I attempt to keep you abreast of the various junctures in Charles and Susie's time line, it is important to keep in mind the dates above as a help to you as you read. This book is a historical/biographical and, therefore, accurate account of Charles and Susie's love story.

Though not necessary to appreciate this book, *Susie: The Life and Legacy of Susannah Spurgeon; Wife of Charles Spurgeon* (Moody Publishers) makes a helpful companion read. In that first book, I peeled back some of the layers of the Spurgeons' marriage, but there is more to tell. In this book, we will gain further insight into the depth of Susie's commitment to Charles and consider how her devotion to him helped to make him the man we admire. We will also see how Charles's love for Susie helped her to become one of Christian history's greatest women. Necessarily, some stories and historical events are repeated in *Yours, till Heaven*. However, these are presented with fresh perspective and are essential to both books. As well, my doctoral thesis, "The Role of Bible Intake and Prayer in the Life of Charles and Susannah Spurgeon" (The Southern Baptist Theological Seminary, 2016), has informed parts of this book, though not extensively.

Charles Spurgeon is primarily referred to in this book as Charles and/or Spurgeon. Susie is referred to as Susie and, occasionally, as Susannah.

Thank you for reading, and I pray that you will be encouraged, and your marriage strengthened, by Charles and Susie's example of abiding love for God and for each other.

Introduction

THE CURTAINS WERE SOON TO FALL on the year 1855 as Charles Spurgeon and Susie Thompson anticipated their January wedding and setting up their first home together as husband and wife. Susie dreamt of their wedding day and imagined theirs would be a marriage made in heaven.[1]

After one last visit before the big day, Charles waved goodbye to Susie and boarded a train for Colchester to spend Christmas with his parents, John and Eliza. Just moments after the train engine lunged forward, Charles's mind was pleasantly distracted by thoughts of his "Sweet One," with her brown eyes and long chestnut curls.[2] Not wasting a second, Charles wielded the "pen of a ready writer" and began a letter to Susie. His thoughts flowed freely onto the paper destined for the hands and eyes of his "Precious Love."[3]

Charles's musings contemplated his life ahead with Susie. He watched the English countryside pass outside the train window and pondered how to best conclude his latest love letter, one that would arrive on Susie's doorstep at Falcon Square a couple weeks prior to their wedding. Never at a loss for the right word, he pressed the nib to paper and signed, "Yours, till Heaven, *and then,*—C. H. S."[4]

Fourteen years later, in 1869, Charles's attention was similarly on his wife. Much had transpired since that cold December day in 1855 when he had written to Susie from the Colchester-bound train: the Surrey Gardens Music Hall was constructed, Charles Darwin announced his theory of evolution in London, the Clock Tower at Westminster (Big Ben) was fully operational, Victoria railway station (and several others) had opened, The Metropolitan Tabernacle was inaugurated, Westminster Palace was rebuilt, and the world's first traffic lights were installed in Parliament Square. Charles was the most popular preacher in the world, and Susie had recovered in Brighton after surgery to help relieve her of chronic gynecological pain.

HEIGHTS OF FAME AND DEPTHS OF LOVE

Between 1855 and 1869, both Charles's and Susie's health had diminished even as Charles's fame as a preacher and author had skyrocketed. A couple things hadn't changed: Charles's love for Susie and his eternal vision. His valediction in a letter to Susie in 1869 was similar to one he penned in 1855: "Yours to love in life and death, and eternally, C. H. S."[5] Neither his popularity nor ill health quenched Charles's sweet expressions of affection for Susie; his love for her only grew through the years, in part because he was purposeful to say *to* her what he felt *for* her. Although he expected their love to change when death took one of them, he never expected it to end.

Thousands clamored to hear Charles preach each week, including political leaders and cultural icons such as President James Garfield, Mark Twain, and Florence Nightingale. It was rumored that even Queen Victoria snuck into a service in disguise to hear the young phenomenon. As a prolific author, Spurgeon penned around one hundred fifty books in addition to his sixty-three volumes of sermons, which still stand as some of the monumental achievements by any Christian leader in history. He was called "the greatest spiritual force of his generation in London, or perhaps in the world."[6] Such accomplishments and praise are just the base of the Spurgeon mountain. However, some of its height is mostly unexplored—such is the case with his marriage to Susie.

SPURGEON: THE GREAT LOVER

With the plethora of labels ("Prince of Preachers," "The Modern Whitefield," etc.) placed upon Charles Spurgeon by authors, his students, and even Susie, there is one never before attached to the famous preacher: the great lover. There you have it. One of the greatest Christian leaders of all time was a great lover at heart. He was a lover of Christ and the lover of one woman, and one woman only, for all his life. Similarly, Susie's love was focused on Christ and on her husband, Charles, exclusively. Indeed, theirs was a love "till Heaven, *and then.*"

The story before you is a love story, a persevering romance set in Victorian times. Yet, to write Spurgeon's romance is, as Susie herself declared, a "sacred and delicate task"[7]—sacred because marriage is, first of all, about Christ and His bride, the church; delicate because it is the closest union into which two people can enter.

The earliest biographies of Spurgeon were bound by "conventional phraseology,"[8] and they had little to say about Charles and Susie's romance. Biographers opted to simply point out a few "common-place details" but concealed what Susie called "the tender truths and sweetness of our mutual love story."[9]

Spurgeon biographer George Lorimer asserted, "Home is, in a peculiar sense, the domain of the wife, and without her consent its sacredness should never be violated."[10] The good news is that Susie gave her consent. She knew that providing such an intimate narrative of her marriage would be considered "unusual" by some. However, she felt that the story should be told.[11] Susie's openness in sharing means that one of the great romances in Christian history is preserved and can serve as an inspiration and encouragement to Christian couples today.

Charles and Susie's love story is a tender narrative. Charles proudly flew a "banner of love" over Susie. He cared little for Victorian privacy in this regard—or in anything else for that matter. "You might write my life across the sky," he said, "I have nothing to conceal."[12] He once told his students that he hated the fashions of society and detested convention.[13] After Susie died, Thomas Spurgeon, in tribute to his mother, wrote: "That [Susie] was a true helpmeet is proved by my dear father's repeated testimony to her worth, by word of mouth and by the fact that he set it down in black and white again and again."[14] A lovely testimony of Charles's unashamed love and respect for Susie—he didn't write of her value once or twice but again and again.

Why shouldn't Charles and Susie's love story be told? There is no marital disunity to hide and no salacious backstory to cover up. Theirs was a public affection that neither were ashamed of. And though we are over 160 years removed from their wedding day, we need Charles and Susie's example. We need to see them as they were and their marriage as it was—warts and all.

They were real people. Their marriage was real. Their story was real—and it *is* relevant. We need to walk with them, hear them as they commune with God and with one another, feel their pain of suffering and loss, peer into their undying devotion to one another, and embrace their eternal vision. They weathered the storms of tragedy, controversy, affliction, separation, and the death of family members and friends, and then their own roads parted with Charles's death preceding Susie's. They both struggled with sin—Spurgeon referenced his "darling sin" of pride,[15] and Susie bemoaned her times of grieving the Holy Spirit.

Charles left behind glimpses of his marriage in his correspondence; but for the details of their love story, we owe most to Susie's writings. In her narrative of their romance, Susie desired that her readers would "gather up with reverent hands, the treasures [she had] thus scattered, and find themselves greatly enriched by their possessions."[16]

Charles believed of his marriage that it was right for him to "value the blessing," but wrong to "make it his all."[17] He urged Christians, whether married or single, not to despise marriage, but also not to seek heaven in it or place it above serving the Lord.[18] The married man, he argued, "will not find it difficult if God hath blessed him with one who will second all his holy endeavours."[19] This reality was essential to the happiness of his marriage to Susie; she supported him and prioritized his ministry pursuits.

Some have suggested that because Charles left Susie for long periods of time to preach and for physical recuperation that he wasn't a great husband, after all. During many of those times, Susie was seriously ill herself. What kind of man does that? Ah, the fog of history clouds our view. Though questions about their relationship are fair, the suggestions are not—unless Charles and Susie's story yields such evidence to the contrary.

Why is there such curiosity still today in a very homely and plainspoken Baptist preacher who lived in the 1800s, especially considering London's esteemed pulpits were occupied with more highly cultured ministers? Why such interest in his wife, Susie, who was an invalid during much of their marriage? Why such curiosity in the two of them as a couple, their marriage, their experiences, and their life and work? Are they a model for modern marriages? Is their love story worth retelling? Why a book such as this?

The answer is that God made Charles and Susie what they were, and, providentially, their influence was of such a nature that it is lasting and large. But they were no ivory tower Christians fit only as museum pieces, looking down from their pedestals. This book, the first of its sort regarding Charles and Susie's marriage, attempts to paint a portrait of the Spurgeons without embellishment.

We will read their words, walk into their world, empathize with them in their sorrows, and rejoice with them in their happiness. We will feel their heartbeat for the poor, for each other, and for God. We will be inspired to join them all these years later in the same good works. And we will learn by their example how to persevere through hardships—physical, mental, and spiritual.

Though we are many years removed from Charles and Susie, the sweetness, commitment, and Christ-centeredness displayed in their marriage is much needed in our own relationships today. As we walk with them from their first meeting until their deaths, we see that though age creases the smooth faces of youth, it need not make ragged the countenance of romance.

CHAPTER 1

SUSIE THOMPSON WAS IN A QUANDARY the first time she laid her eyes upon Charles Spurgeon; she didn't know whether to laugh or cry. She simply couldn't imagine why others at New Park Street Chapel (NPSC) were enthused by the nineteen-year-old country preacher. Nothing about the young man impressed her—not his hair, his clothes, his accent, or even his preaching. Fast-forward just eight months, and Susie is weeping tears of joy that Charles Spurgeon had just declared his love and asked her to marry him.

How did the citified Susannah Thompson ever develop an interest in the rural and unpolished Charles Spurgeon? Two-and-a-half years his senior, she was, by all descriptions, lovely in appearance and refined in demeanor. There must have been many city boys vying for her attention, from London, where she lived, to Paris, where she frequently traveled. Susie was "small and pretty in a quiet way, with a mass of brown curls and a singularly sweet smile."[1] Charles on the other hand was "short, plump, and carelessly dressed, with protruding teeth and eyes that did not quite match."[2] Some people considered him unattractive, a verdict with which he readily agreed. However, Charles's friends viewed him differently, appreciating not only his spiritual fervency and mental prowess but also "his twinkling, humorous eyes, his mellow voice, and the charm and graciousness of his personality."[3]

Charles and Susie were both Englanders but from two different cultures—as different as the rural Stambourne Meeting House (where Charles's grandfather ministered) was from London's St. Paul's Cathedral, towering majestically over the landscape. In Charles and Susie, country and city meshed, and the merging of their lives is their love story.

Charles arrived in London by train on Saturday, December 17, 1853, the day before he was to preach at the NPSC as a guest preacher. The church had been without a pastor for some time and was in steep decline.

London's bustling metropolis overwhelmed Charles from the moment he stepped off of the train and his feet hit the ground. He longed to be back at his church in Waterbeach and his apartment in Cambridge, some seventy miles north. The country air he usually breathed was a stark contrast to the industrial smog of London's waste-filled streets. God had blessed Waterbeach Baptist Chapel with conversions and numerical growth—from about forty people when Charles arrived to around four hundred, and this over the span of only two years. In this regard, the village church was in much better circumstances than the historic city congregation.

The night before he preached, Charles tossed and turned in the tiny room of the dingy and clamoring boarding house in Queen

Square, Bloomsbury, just north of the NPSC. The church's hospitality had left much to be desired in sending him to such a place. Living in the metropolis of the world and marrying a refined London girl were the furthest things from Charles's mind. His objective was to preach on Sunday and then rush back to his village church as quickly as possible. Outside, it was a typical winter's evening in London—cold, damp, and cloudy, three things that worked against Spurgeon's health throughout most of his years there.

Across town at 7 St. Ann's Terrace, Brixton Road, Susie Thompson was cozy in the spacious home she and her parents shared with her uncle, aunt, and their children. She rested comfortably while, a couple miles away, the flickering gas lights and noisy streets just outside of Charles's window kept his sleep at bay. Prior to retiring to his room earlier that evening, Charles had been playfully mocked by some of the other residents of the boarding house for his thick Essex accent and his less-than-dapper appearance. They wagged their tongues and shook their heads as they imagined the young and countrified Spurgeon preaching in a city of polite and educated preachers. Little did they know what awaited NPSC, the city of London, and the world as a result of young Spurgeon's visit that weekend. Spurgeon biographer H. I. Wayland writes,

> If anyone had predicted that the young rustic would begin on the next day a ministry of thirty-eight years in the metropolis of the civilized world, a ministry unsurpassed in the history of Christendom; and that at last he would be borne to his grave with the burial of a king, the words would have seemed as idle tales, made of the same stuff as the wildest of the Arabian Nights.[4]

Susie was aware that the NPSC was hosting the "Boy Preacher of the Fens"; however, she had little interest in hearing him, and she skipped the morning service. Susie and her parents had mostly lost interest in the church since the pastor they loved, James Smith, had resigned and the church had declined. It took a bit of persuasion from respected friends Thomas and Unity Olney to convince her to attend the Sunday evening service.[5]

Both Susie *and* Charles were surprised that he was ever invited to preach at the historic church that had once been served by the likes of Benjamin Keach, John Gill, and John Rippon—three legendary pastors. Charles couldn't imagine why the esteemed London church wanted him, a mere country preacher, to fill their pulpit. In fact, when the invitation had arrived in the mail some weeks earlier, Charles thought the letter had been addressed to the wrong Spurgeon.

Susie had similar doubts, and her first impression of Charles did nothing to assuage her concerns. When she first saw and heard him preach, she was shocked that the uncouth, poorly groomed, and unfashionably dressed country boy was standing in the pulpit of the prestigious church. However, church leaders did not share Susie's sentiments, and, concerned about the future of NPSC, they invited the young preacher back numerous times. They rested their hope for church renewal on Charles. Susie just shook her head.

Spurgeon was formally installed as pastor of NPSC in April of 1854. Though young, he was a throwback to an era quickly fading away filled with conscience-piercing preachers such as William Jay and John Angell James. Perhaps more surprising than Charles Spurgeon's installation as pastor was the romance between Charles and Susie that unfolded soon afterward. The two became well acquainted as their individual visits to the home of Thomas and Unity coincided.

Charles ascertained that Susie was unsettled spiritually. Her conversion, just over a year earlier in late 1852, was accompanied by troublesome doubts. Charles reached out to her in hopes of encouraging her in her faith. When a parcel from Charles containing *The Pilgrim's Progress* reached her home, Susie was curious and surprised.

Outside of the Bible itself, Charles was most helped in his Christian pilgrimage by John Bunyan's classic allegory of the Christian life. Rarely was Charles further than arm's reach from a copy of Bunyan's book, a book he felt might also reassure Susie.

This was a turning point in their evolving friendship. Neither Charles nor his preaching offended Susie any longer, and she now considered his ministry just what she desperately needed. As Susie thumbed through the pages of *The Pilgrim's Progress*, she was impressed by Charles's thoughtfulness in giving her a "precious" and "helpful" gift.[6] Trembling, Susie met with Charles and detailed to him her vexatious spiritual situation. Charles was gentle in his counsel, leading her to a deeper faith in Christ.[7]

On June 10, less than two months after his installation as pastor, Charles revealed to Susie his growing affection for her, strongly hinting that he imagined a future together. This he did, in cleverness typical to him, by pointing her to a passage on marriage in Martin Tupper's book *Proverbial Philosophy* and asking her if she prayed for her future husband. The message was clear, surprising, and welcomed by Susie. Two months later, on August 2, Charles proposed to Susie in her grandparents' quaint little garden. Susie was delighted, and the unlikely couple was engaged. A bit of historical and cultural context is helpful in further understanding why Charles and Susie were such an "unlikely couple."

Susie Thompson's parents, Robert and Susannah, were married April 6, 1831, in London by "banns," indicating that they were likely poor.[8] On January 15, 1832, nine months after their wedding, their first and only child, Susie, was born. Eventually finances improved for the Thompson family, though with times of noticeable and nearly devastating downfalls.

That same year ushered in developments in their world that were later important to Susie and her parents, as well as to Charles Spurgeon. Carter Lane Baptist Church, where the hymn writer and author John Rippon was then pastor and the Thomas Olney family maintained their church membership, moved to New Park Street, south of the Thames and in the neighborhood where Shakespeare's Globe Theatre had once stood. The church's new location was also near where John Bunyan had preached during his London visits, and near the Marshalsea prison, where the father of Charles Dickens was incarcerated in 1824 for indebtedness.

With the move, the church was renamed New Park Street Chapel. Susie and her parents were regular attendees of the NPSC by the 1840s. This was the name and location of the church when Charles first preached there in December 1853.

Though middle-class Victorian homes were stocked with literature from popular novelists such as Dickens or Thackeray, staple Christian books in Susie's home likely included a King James Version of the Bible, *Foxe's Book of Martyrs*, *The Book of Common Prayer*, and some guide to morning and evening devotions. Susie almost certainly read the collection of brief devotional sermons, *The Book That Will Suit You; or A Word for Every One*, by her pastor James Smith. Though her childhood was not as robustly saturated with deep theology as Charles's, she, like most Victorian children, had a religious upbringing.

Susie strolled down city streets lined with architectural marvels and bustling with activity—from merchants selling wine and tea, to factory workers laboring in often dark and dangerous conditions just to survive. She had to maneuver around mud and horse manure as she crossed roads, not yet shoveled and swept by the ever-present street cleaners. Susie's London was beautiful and dirty, smoky and dangerous, and prosperous and poor. Its roads were traveled by politicians and orphans, high-society ladies wearing hats and carrying parasols in the daytime and 8,600 women engaged in prostitution at night.[9] And, London was noisy with "the incessant sound of wheels and horses' hooves clacking over the pavement . . . the bell of the muffin man, and the cries of street peddlers selling such items as dolls, matches, books, knives, eels, pens, rat poison, key rings, eggs and china."[10]

CHARLES'S EARLY RURAL EXPERIENCES

In contrast to Susie's urban upbringing, Charles was born in a small town, and for most of his first nineteen years, he was a boy of the deep country. It was not primarily London that made the great preacher but it was Essex's villages and towns: Stambourne where his grandparents lived, the small town of Colchester in his later childhood and early youth with his parents, and Cambridge's spires and neighboring areas in his mid and later teenage years that helped to form the fabric of Charles's character.

London had its place in shaping the man whose stature towered during his lifetime, but to unearth the context of Charles Spurgeon, one must depart from the city, walk the dirt roads of the countryside, and sit beneath the trees in the green pastures of Stambourne. One must then climb into the dimly lit attic of pastor James Spurgeon, Charles's grandfather, and examine the rustic old Puritan volumes as Charles himself often did, running his fingers across the bindings even before he could read them. From the shelves of that attic library, nestled somewhere between the writings of Thomas Brooks and Boswell's biography of Samuel Johnson, one must then survey *The Pilgrim's Progress,* penned by John Bunyan, the tinker from nearby Bedford. Bunyan was important to Charles, not only because of his classic allegory, but also because he wrote it while imprisoned for preaching the gospel without license from the Established Church. From boyhood, Charles revered Christians who had heroically suffered for their faith. His admiration sprung in part from reading *Foxe's Book of Martyrs* and learning later that his distant relative Job Spurgeon had, many years prior, been imprisoned for attending a non-sanctioned church meeting.

The village of Bedford, where Bunyan had ministered, was not far removed from the path winding along the green countryside from Stambourne to Colchester, where Charles's parents John and Eliza Spurgeon resided. It was bloodstained Puritan soil, Puritan books, a Puritan-like grandfather, and godly parents who, in large part, molded the child Charles.

Whereas Susie enjoyed the progressing city with its industry, shops, modern inventions, and historic monuments, Charles's world was meandering country paths and country preachers—a more innocent world mostly untouched by the Industrial Revolution. After Charles married Susie, he sought to recreate the world of his youth on a smaller scale. With the exception of their first residence, subsequent homes had gardens, a fernery, and even milk cows.

A BIBLE ON THE TABLE
OF EVERY VICTORIAN HOME

Victorianism characterized most of the nineteenth century, into the early part of the twentieth. It was a time of progress in industry and technology, and London was the seat of its advancement, not only in England but also the world. Early to mid-Victorianism was challenging as people crowded London, seeking opportunities with the Industrial Revolution. Cholera outbreaks and financial disaster befell many of the great city's inhabitants. London smog and London fog were real and problematic for residents. At their worst from November through February, they were often yellow and thick, creating darkness during the daytime and requiring residents and business owners to light lamps. This extended beyond the city for several miles into the suburbs. Numerous health problems resulted—in part from the black smoke that ascended from "thousands of coal fires."[11] There are accounts of people getting lost in the fogs, inadvertently walking into the Thames and drowning.[12]

From the work of famous art critic John Ruskin to the stories of celebrity novelist Dickens, the Victorians were "awash in texts"; but, as scholar Timothy Larsen argues, they were a people of "one book"—the Bible.[13] It was into this world that Charles Spurgeon and Susie Thompson were born, a world later overrun with novels, magazines, newspapers, and other literature—but, at least on the surface, a world that was most known literarily by the Bible. The Bible was the standard text in Victorian schools, and it was a staple in every home where morning and evening devotions were generally practiced. Larsen notes that even the "polemical agnostic T. H. Huxley threw his strong support behind the Bible as a primary text in the core curriculum for elementary school children—it was the Bible first, then 'reading, writing, and arithmetic.'"[14]

Even a cursory glance at the volumes of Victorian authors reveals the importance of Scripture in their writings. Take Charles Spurgeon's friend John Ruskin, one not known for his commitment to orthodox Christian doctrine. His writings inspired a three-hundred-page book, *The Bible References of John Ruskin* (1898).[15] References to Scripture abounded in the literature of Victorianism, from the Christian poet Christina Rossetti to the atheist P. B. Shelley. Charles Dickens's religious outlook lacked doctrinal precision, and his moral choices sometimes caused the pious to wince, but he was one who nevertheless believed that every Victorian should be familiar with the Bible.[16]

Providentially, Charles and Susie were born at a time of growing literary interests and publishing that eventually assisted both of them with their own prolific writing careers. And while the Bible may have fascinated many people in England, it was the singular influence in the lives of Charles and Susie. When Charles Spurgeon burst upon the scene with a Bible in his hand that he believed and preached, there was a spiritual revival in the churches and an awakening in the city.

ENGAGEMENT YEARS AND MARRIAGE

During Charles and Susie's engagement (August 1854 to January 1856), they became better acquainted in the midst of Charles's busy ministry. They didn't engage in the types of activities enjoyed by the upper classes, such as balls and other social events. Even if Charles and Susie had held the societal status that would garner an invitation to a ball, Charles was opposed to dancing. But they found sufficient happiness in just being together. They met once a week at the Crystal Palace, and walked in public, hand-in-hand;

they even made a trip to Colchester together to meet Charles's extended family.

When Charles and Susie were married on January 8, 1856, their wedding ceremony was not an elaborate one, despite Charles's growing popularity. Instead it was the common morning service for a nonconformist Christian couple in 1856 Victorian England. The Scriptures were read, the gospel was proclaimed, and the minister blessed the couple. After the wedding, it was customary for couples to visit with the bride's family for a celebratory breakfast prepared by the bride's mother.[17] Though Susie's wedding dress is nowhere described, there were norms concerning wedding attire.

> White gowns did not become especially common until
> the 1870s; most middle-class brides were married in
> a colored dress. It would be new for the wedding but
> made in a style that could be used for going to church
> and making calls during the following year. Pastels were
> sometimes preferred, but other wedding dresses seen in
> museums are bronze taffeta, wine velvet, and deep purple
> silk. Whatever the color of her dress, the bride wore a
> delicate white veil covering her head and upper body.[18]

Susie may have even worn an orange blossom wreath on her head, traditional from 1840.[19]

Charles and Susie's wedding, though simple, nevertheless took on a life of its own, exceeding in attendance and energy, if not in pomp and circumstance, the weddings of the courtly in Victorian culture. This was not by design, but simply a result of Spurgeon's popularity by that time. It seemed that everyone in London was interested in their wedding. Newspapers carried the story as thousands of curiosity seekers thronged the streets on that damp and foggy morning. The chapel itself was packed beyond capacity with

2,000 people in attendance; some five hundred ladies arrived hours before the doors opened in hopes of securing excellent seating. Extra policemen were commissioned to patrol as people pressed for just a glimpse of the bride and groom and their wedding party. All of this for a simple Baptist preacher and his bride-to-be—it almost seems hard to believe. But many of Charles and Susie's experiences together defy imagination. Susie was not swayed by all of the attention that day; she simply said, "God Himself united our hearts in indissoluble bonds of true affection and gave us to each other forever." She was happy.[20]

After Susie cut the wedding cake and the breakfast at her parents' home was finished, the newlyweds departed for Paris for their ten-day honeymoon. There, Susie, fluent in French and well acquainted with the city from her earlier travels, delighted her new husband and first-time visitor to the City of Light as his tour guide to the majestic cathedrals, art galleries, and historical sites of Paris.

The gleeful young couple were free from any consciousness of the future and all of the challenges that it would bring. Charles and Susie laughed, touched, and strolled the streets together in romantic Paris. They were jubilant. Upon visiting Sainte Chapelle, Charles thought the stained glass was heavenly. Susie agreed: "Its loveliness looked almost celestial, as we stood enwrapped in its radiance, the light of the sinking sun glorifying its matchless windows into a very dream of dazzling grace and harmony of colour."[21]

The couple would carry the spirit of that splendor into the next phase of their journey together.

Upon returning to London, Susie set up their first home together at 217 New Kent Road, very near where Susie was born and not far from NPSC and from the future Metropolitan Tabernacle. Susie "admired everything in the house"[22] and considered it "delightful."

Charles prayed for God's blessing on their simple little home.[23] The house had three stories with several rooms, the best room was on the second floor and it was set aside, at Susie's insistence, as Charles's study.[24] On the third floor, just above the study, twin boys, Charles Jr. and Thomas, were welcomed on September 20, 1856. Such marked the happy days of the first year of Charles and Susie's marriage.

Charles and Susie had a joyful marriage, but not an effortless one. But for the newlyweds, future complications were unknown as they reveled in one another's love. They were allowed a blissful but brief season of unhindered happiness before storm clouds of trouble rolled into their home. Susie later wrote, "The strongest saint, the firmest believer, would never dare to gaze upon the untrodden pathway which lies before him; and we thank God that He has put such knowledge utterly out of our reach."[25]

Heights of fame and depths of suffering came to their doorstep in short order. However, Charles and Susie had a robust spirituality, cultivated by spiritual disciplines, that steeled them against the dangers of popularity and heartbreaking tragedy and helped them to thrive in their marriage and ministry.

CHAPTER 2

WHEN CHARLES PROPOSED MARRIAGE TO SUSIE in August of 1854, she admitted to being very nervous and speechless. After accepting his proposal, she quickly found a quiet place upstairs in her grandparents' home where she fell to her knees, and, with tears streaming down her cheeks, she lifted her voice heavenward in praise and thanksgiving to God "for his great mercy in giving me the love of so good a man."[1] Her first inclination was to pray. This proclivity toward prayer remained with her for the rest of her life.

Susie discerned enough of Charles's popularity, giftedness, and gospel-singularity to realize that he was no ordinary man; however, neither she nor anyone else envisioned that the interest then surrounding her fiancé would steadily grow during their thirty-six-year marriage. He was no shooting star who would fall with a thud on the London landscape. Charles was famous early in his London

ministry in 1854, and his death in 1892 provoked the prayers of a
nation and the tears of the world. The shoes that Susie was called to
fill required a spirituality that was drilled down deep into the well of
God's truth and grace. Both Charles and Susie had to cast their burdens and their successes upon the Lord if they were to faithfully and
perseveringly walk the pathway that God had marked out for them.

After they were married, Susie frequently sat in Charles's
study when he was away from home. Thousands of volumes lined
his shelves untouched. Always a voracious reader, Charles's books
were as friends. From childhood, he was fascinated not only by the
contents of books but also by their design. Susie knew Charles's
books well—from personal perusal and reading as well as assisting
Charles in his studies. As she sat at his table, her gaze fell upon
his closed inkstand, his unused pens, and his organized papers. All
indicated to Susie that he would not be back soon. She surveyed
her beloved's sacred space and felt his absence. Lonely and worried,
Susie confessed her inadequacy of carrying such a hefty load—of
being the wife of a famed preacher and of being alone—except for
the "given grace to commit all into the Father's loving hand, and
the granted faith to believe that 'He hath done all things well.'"[2]

Charles was conflicted over his absences from Susie. He contemplated: "It would be a great pity if a man never spent five minutes
with his wife, but was forced to always be hard at work."[3] Charles
spent time with Susie, but he recognized the demands of his ministry came with a cost to her—and to him. During their engagement, he had not been as sensitive to her feelings in this regard. But
later, his travels outside of London evoked another perspective: "I
can now thoroughly sympathize with your tears, because I feel in
no little degree that pang of absence which my constant engage-
ments prevented me from noticing when in London."[4] Despite the

extraordinary circumstances that Charles's fame brought to their home, the couple's piety prevented them from wilting beneath the hot sun of their trials.

On their knees with an open Bible, Charles and Susie's spirituality deepened and steeled them for their journey together. Both recognized the emptiness of popularity and marriage without God's help. Charles said that even having Susie's sweet love was insufficient if he should "be left of God to fall, and to depart from His ways." The same was true of his success. "I tremble at the giddy height on which I stand, and could wish myself unknown, for indeed I am unworthy of all my honours and my fame."[5]

To know God as He is revealed in the Bible and to walk closely with Him was the essence of Charles and Susie's spirituality. A desire to know and follow God motivated them in the spiritual disciplines of Bible reading, prayer, family and congregational worship, and meditation on Scripture. True spirituality was a matter of joyful obedience *and* the necessary glue that cemented the Spurgeons' love and hopeful outlook even when the high waves of controversy, sickness, and loss crashed heavily upon them.

They enjoyed an experiential piety—a godliness of loving intimacy with God displayed in holiness of life. It was a way of life that Charles and Susie practiced and impressed upon their sons. Susie once wrote her son Thomas, when he was a student in Brighton, about a prayer meeting that he was attending. Her desire was that God would bless the meeting and protect it from becoming "a mere formal service" but that it might have "loving, earnest, pleading hearts to keep it alive, and well pleasing to the Lord."[6]

Pious practices, and even proficiency in theology, absent of love were profitless.

LEARNING ABOUT SPIRITUALITY
FROM OTHERS

Both Charles and Susie's conversion to Christ occurred after their formative childhood years. However, the people, places, and books that they encountered in their earlier days established patterns of godliness that later served them well.

Bible reading and preaching were plentiful in Charles's boyhood experiences. His grandfather James and his father, John, were both gospel preachers, and his grandmother Sarah and mother, Eliza, were godly examples to him. John Spurgeon was a hardworking bi-vocational pastor, and due to his full schedule, he trusted daily religious training of their children to Eliza. The road had been rough for John and Eliza; nine of their seventeen children died in infancy. Their strong faith in Christ and vibrant godliness sustained them through many a trying time.

Eliza prayed ardently for her children, read the Bible to them, and encouraged them to read evangelistic literature. Charles thanked God for making him the son of a mother who prayed "*for*" him and "*with*" him.[7] Many people surmised as to the success of Charles. He said, "I can tell you two reasons why I am what I am . . . My mother, and the truth of my message."[8] Charles was not unlike some of his heroes from history who had praying mothers.

Though Charles was blessed with a godly family, it was a stranger, a scarcely educated Methodist itinerant, who was the instrument of his salvation. January 6, 1850, Charles was diverted by a snowstorm through the doors of a Primitive Methodist chapel. There he heard a simple message exhorting him to "look unto Christ."[9]

After his conversion, Charles's passion for God's Word blazed with energy.

"How beautiful is the Bible!" he wrote to his father. "I never loved it so before; it seems to me as necessary food. I feel that I have not one particle of spiritual life in me but what the Spirit placed there."[10] Those were delightful words to his father's ears.

Around the time of his baptism in May of 1850, he wrote his mother: "You, my Mother have been the great means in God's hand of rendering me what I hope I am. Your kind, warning, Sabbath-evening addresses were too deeply settled on my heart to be forgotten. You, by God's blessings, prepared the way for the preached Word."[11]

Susie's childhood story and early spiritual influences are more shrouded in mystery than Charles's. She wrote little about her parents, leaving behind only a few paragraphs about her mother and only a couple of fragments regarding her father. The absence of information about her parents is curious but, as previously stated, they were active attendees with Susie at the New Park Street Chapel in the 1840s.[12]

Susie was converted in late 1852 when Rev. S. B. Bergne of the Poultry Chapel expounded Romans chapter 10. However, it was later, in the spring of 1854, that she was assured of salvation through Charles Spurgeon's ministry to her. From that point forward the Bible was Susie's source of spiritual nourishment. She wrote of her desire to sit at God's table each morning and "eat and drink abundantly, as Thy beloved ones may do."[13] Eating and drinking at the Lord's table meant reading and meditating on the Bible.

The Puritans and George Whitefield as Influences

The writings of a diverse group of Christian leaders from history left their mark on Charles and Susie. Charles was greatly helped by the God-centered theology and practical piety of the English

Puritans and the Great Awakening evangelist, George Whitefield. From childhood, under the tutelage of his grandfather and father, Charles had imbibed Puritan writings. Later he settled on George Whitefield as his hero.

It's not hard to imagine that these two perspectives (the Puritans and Whitefield) regarding marriage, ministry, and spirituality helped Charles to maintain balance in his private, domestic, and ministerial duties. He often felt torn between home responsibilities and work, but his historical heroes left patterns, both positive and negative, that he could emulate and/or avoid.

Charles's romantic expressions to Susie are similar to the musings of Puritan pastor Thomas Hooker.

> The man whose heart is endeared to the woman he loves ... dreams of her in the night, hath her in his eye and apprehension when he awakes, museth on her as he sits at the table, walks with her when he travels. ... She lies in his bosom, and his heart trusts in her, which forceth all to confess that the stream of his affection, like a mighty current, runs with full tide and strength.[14]

Few Christian leaders in history have more beautifully expressed their romantic feelings for their lover than Charles Spurgeon. Apparently, reading the Puritans helped him in that regard.

Yet Charles was also singularly devoted to his public ministry—a devotion that was likely influenced not only by the Puritans but by George Whitefield, especially. Whitefield's preaching ministry left its mark on London—and all of England and America. Charles emulated Whitefield's personal piety, evangelistic zeal, and ministry commitment. He asserted, "My own model, if I may have such a thing in due subordination to my Lord, is George Whitefield;

but with unequal footsteps must I follow in his glorious track."[15]

Spurgeon, like Whitefield, was indefatigable in his work ethic.[16] Just weeks after his marriage, Whitefield wrote: "I trust I was married *in the* LORD; and as I married for him, I trust I shall thereby not be hindered, but rather forwarded in my work. O for that blessed time when we shall neither marry nor be given in marriage but be as the angels of GOD! My soul longs for that glorious season."[17] This example, Charles followed to an extent; but where Whitefield's marriage was lacking in expressive affection, Charles's marriage flourished.

When it came to romance, Spurgeon, the great lover, was more Puritan than Whitefield, and Susie couldn't have been happier. Charles and Susie's marriage was founded on fundamental biblical principles exemplified by those people who were most influential in their lives—their family, historical heroes, and personal acquaintances.

The Center as My Sun

As important as family, Christian leaders, and books were to Charles and Susie, the depth of their devotion to God is evident by the centrality of Christ in their thinking, writing, and practices. Charles wrote,

> A man who is a believing admirer and a hearty lover of
> the truth, as it is in Jesus, is in a right place to follow
> with advantage any other branch of science. . . . Once
> when I read books, I put all my knowledge together in
> glorious confusion; but ever since I have known Christ, I
> have put Christ in the centre as my sun, and each science
> revolves around it like a planet, while minor sciences are
> satellites to these planets.[18]

The Spurgeons' marriage revolved around Jesus. Where did Charles look for guidance as a husband? He looked to Jesus: "The true Christian is to be such a husband as Christ was to his spouse."[19] A Christocentric reading of the Scripture informed Charles that he was to love Susie in a "special," "constant," "enduring," and "delighted" manner, for he took Christ as his Savior, his model, and his teacher.[20] And Susie felt that she was married to a man who loved her deeply because he loved Christ supremely. Susie's marriage caused her to marvel at "the mercy of my God."[21] Charles marveled at the depth of Susie's spirituality.[22] Both marveled at the glory of Christ.

Susie encouraged readers of her book *Ten Years After!* to envision God's care through the lens of Christ. She knew that spiritual nourishment was found "*in Christ*, in *Christ's life in thee*," for in Him there is "a never-failing spring of comfort and renewing grace, which no heat of sorrow, or scorching wind of earthly care, can ever dry up."[23]

Charles hadn't experienced life with an ungodly wife: "I have never tasted of such bitter herbs, but I pity from my very heart those who have this diet [of a complaining wife] every day of their lives."[24] Rather than offering "bitter herbs," Susie was Charles's "delighted companion." She expressed "heartfelt gratitude to God" that she was "permitted to encircle him with all the comforting care and tender affection which it was in a wife's power to bestow."[25] The delightfulness in Charles and Susie's marriage was inseparable from their Christ-centered piety.

GOD'S WORD ON HOW TO LOVE

Charles and Susie's Christ-centered perspective was honed through their disciplined reading of the Bible. Their approach was simple—they believed the Bible to be true, trustworthy, and sufficient because of the infallibility of God Himself. And, trusting in the reliability of the Bible—they read it faithfully, confidently, and expectantly. Everything that they needed to know about God and about how to love one another was contained in the Bible. Charles imagined that if the words in the Bible were merely constructions of men, then they might be quickly discarded. However, he believed the Bible to be "God's handwriting" and, therefore, authoritative.[26] Susie said that it was "well to ponder every weighty sentence" of God's "loving voice."[27]

Why was Bible reading so important to Charles? He said that it was through the Bible that God speaks to His people.[28] Charles wrote prolifically, producing books of sermons, commentaries on Scripture, and aids to family worship. Yet he bristled at the thought that any of his books (or anyone else's) might substitute for one's reading of Scripture. Books were valuable to one's growth in godliness, but Charles desired that Christians dig deeply into the Bible itself. "If the heavenly gold is not worth digging for, you are not likely to discover it."[29] Daily, when Charles and Susie read the Bible, they heard the voice of God speaking from the words contained therein. The Bible was the foundation upon which their marriage stood, and it was the wisdom from which their marriage prospered.

Taking the Bible to Heart

On many Saturdays, Charles and Susie hosted students at their home, Westwood. They moved to this house in the Beulah Hill neighborhood of southeast London in 1880, and it was their last home together before Charles died in 1892. Not even a hundred yards from the house and just down a grassy slope and not far from their little pond was a tree they named "The Question Oak."

It was beneath the outstretched branches of that aged tree that Charles, and sometimes Susie, met with students and answered their questions.

Charles's students affectionately referred to him as "the Governor." On one occasion, a student asked him: "Do you advise the systematic and consecutive reading of the Bible, rather than a meditation upon special portions of the Word?" Charles turned to Susie: "Wifey can tell you about that," he said, "for she has read the Book *through* many times."

"How many times have you gone through the Bible, wifey?"

"Fourteen times, which means reading about three chapters daily to accomplish this in a year."

"Do you recommend the plan?"

"On some accounts, I do; it makes one acquainted with the historical and prophetic portions of God's Word which otherwise might be passed over, and it gives a more general knowledge of the whole Book; but for spiritual enlightenment and refreshment, I cannot commend it."

"Why do you practice it then, wifey?"

"It has become a habit with me, and I do not like to give it up: but I often get more comfort and blessing out of half a verse, when applied by the Spirit of God, than from the three chapters, which are more likely to be read as a duty, rather than a pleasure."

Addressing his students again, Charles said:

"Now, gentleman, I would advise you to stick to your texts, and suck all the sweetness out of each one, before you proceed to another. The bees in my garden always load up with all they can carry away from every blossom; they don't get a sip here, and a dust of pollen there, but they ransack each flower thoroughly, and I think you will do well to follow their example."[30]

For Charles and Susie, meditation was the filling of their minds with Scripture: Scripture thought upon, pondered, considered, prayed over. Meditation was not a passive, mind-emptying, or mystical exercise for Charles and Susie; it involved actively marshaling all of their intellectual resources so as to make "sweet truth" of Scripture accessible. Charles proclaimed, "These grapes [Bible passages] will yield no wine until we tread on them."[31] Meditation was treading on the words of Scripture—pressing out from them the truth about everything that God taught for the purpose of knowing and walking with God.

PRAYER—A MOST PRECIOUS THING

If one were transported back in time to Charles and Susie's home and allowed to walk beside them throughout their day, they would be struck both by the brevity and the frequency of their prayers. Prayer was "a most precious thing" in the Spurgeons' home because it brought them into communion with God and channeled inestimable blessings from God to them.[32]

Their faith was simple—they asked God for whatever they needed and trusted that He would supply. Charles believed that God gave promises in the Bible with intent to fulfill said promises to those who asked by faith. He was not advocating for what is today commonly called a prosperity gospel. Quite the opposite; he earnestly read the Bible in context and searched for God's promises. Discovering them, he asked God to fulfill His promises. Very simply, Charles and Susie prayed expectantly that God, out of His generous kindness and love, would act on their behalf.

When Susie's mind and body were taxed, she looked "entreatingly to Him who alone could move brain, and heart, and hand."[33] Though she leaned on her husband for help, she recognized that the source of her ultimate support for every task was the Lord. Sometimes Susie's prayers were unuttered; they were merely her glances upward with longing eyes. Prayer was her direct line to God—"*a telephone from my lips to thy heart and every sigh is recorded there.*"[34] Susie didn't view God as reluctant to hear her prayers for He had invited her to approach Him with a sense of boldness.

Charles prayed spontaneously, and he prayed in connection with his Bible reading. He asked his church members, "Do you wish to begin to be true readers? Will you henceforth labor to understand?" He answered, "Then you must get to your knees. You must cry to God for direction." This was Charles's practice, and he found that prayer was a means of "soul enrichment" and "the vessel which trades with heaven, and comes home from the celestial country laden with treasures."[35] In Spurgeon's thinking, each of the spiritual disciplines build on and complement one another. Pray to understand Scripture, read Scripture to understand prayer, and meditate on Scripture to internalize its truths and to consider how to apply God's Word in every area of life.

Charles and Susie prayed privately, together, and with others. "Happy is the household, which meets every morning for prayer! Happy are they who let not the evening depart without uniting in supplication!"[36] Charles practiced what he preached. Peter Morden writes,

> His [Spurgeon's] basic pattern was to pray morning
> and evening . . . Sometimes he would pray with his

family ... sometimes he would be alone. But his prayer life certainly did not stop there; Spurgeon wanted to maintain continued communion with God throughout the day. One of the ways he sought to do this was by praying short, one-sentence prayers as he went about his daily work ... These short, pithy prayers are what have been called "arrow prayers", prayers addressed to God in the midst of a day full of all sorts of different tasks.[37]

While in prayer, Charles and Susie were in communion with God. They sought help from God, and they asked for understanding into God's Word so that they might know how to walk faithfully with God.

As Susie knelt in prayer early in the morning, she felt it was so easy to "hate sin and dwell in Him" that she could almost look forward to facing the day's trials, knowing they could be overcome.[38] However, as she left the mercy seat of prayer and entered into her work for the day, she felt the challenge of keeping God in her thoughts. She was transparent concerning her struggle with sin and her remedy was to pray and walk in the Spirit and to ask for God's help. She prayed, "Blessed Jesus, put forth Your hand, and take Your poor, silly, fluttering dove into the ark of Your love!" She imagined a spiritual revival if every Christian brought into their thoughts, words, and deeds the joy of communion with God. Such would lead them to more carefully follow after God.[39] She was no mere theoretician; she knew what it was to battle with sin, and prayer and Scripture meditation were but two of her weapons in what Bunyan called the "Holy War."[40]

Charles and Susie prayed together "as joint heirs of grace" because "any temper of habit, which hinders this, is evil" and indicative of a pilotless household.[41] Charles, directly connected the effectiveness of his prayers to his love and honor for Susie.[42] During a particular season in Charles's life, he felt cold toward God—and he was not content in his coldness. So he fought, by prayer, for spiritual heat—for passion—for fervent joy in Christ. He knew that in Susie he had a praying wife, one who believed, as he did, that when God blesses His people, He always uses the prayers of His people. "Pray for me, my love; and may our united petitions win a blessing through the Saviour's merit."[43] She responded to that particular request with a benediction: "May His blessing rest in an especial manner on you to-night, my dearly-beloved."[44]

This was the atmosphere of Charles and Susie's marriage—prayer was no unusual practice; it was the very oxygen that they breathed.

On a particular, but characteristic occasion, Charles was lonely, discouraged, and longing for Susie. However, since she was miles away, he wrote her a letter and said he would "go upstairs alone, and pour out my griefs into my Saviour's ear."[45] Another time, he wrote that Susie was sweet to him and that, though he was fighting sleep, he planned to stay awake to ask God to bless her.[46] In yet another correspondence, he urged Susie to pray even as he confessed his spiritual inadequacy: "I shall feel deeply indebted to you if you will pray very earnestly for me. I fear I am not so full of love to God as I used to be. I lament my sad decline in spiritual things."[47]

Charles and Susie enjoyed communion with God, and that led them to real communion with one another. Real communion in marriage is honest communion. Real communion is built on trust and confidence. This is the picture of a healthy marriage: the husband prays for his wife, the wife prays for her husband, and both pray together. And in that, there is a raw honesty that is safe. The husband or wife fears no loss of love, respect, care, or presence when they open their hearts and pour out their sins, their heartbreaks, their joys, and their sorrows. Why? They know that on the other side of the conversation is a partner who loves them, who is working for their best interests, and who will bring them before the throne of God in prayer. Charles and Susie's marriage thrived on freedom to ask for help and to expect the other to respond lovingly.

A LEGACY OF FAMILY WORSHIP

The practice of family worship was etched on Charles's heart from infancy by his parents and grandparents. Appropriate to her consistency in Bible reading and prayer, his grandmother died reading Scripture:

> One Sunday morning . . . she remarked to her old husband
> that she did not feel well, and would stay at home and
> read her Bible and pray, while he preached. On his return
> he found her in the old armchair, her Bible spread out on
> her lap, her spectacles across it, her head bowed upon her
> breast, still in death. And her finger rested upon Job xix,
> 21: "The hand of God hath touched me."[48]

Within their marriage—though Susie was a faithful instrument of piety in the home, reading, praying for, and singing with her children—Charles ensured that Scripture and prayer permeated family life. In his book *The Interpreter*, Charles explained that family devotional time is one of the "greatest of Christian institutions." Like his Puritan heroes, he "would sooner have omitted a meal than have given up morning or evening prayers." He considered neglecting family worship an evil.[49]

Susie had fond memories of evening devotional exercises. She recalled "bright, witty, and always interesting" conversation during teatime. After the meal, everyone in their home, guests, servants, and family, retreated to Charles's study. There, Susie said, "My beloved's prayers were remarkable for their tender childlikeness, their spiritual pathos, and their intense devotion." She remembered Charles coming "as near to God as a little child to a loving father." The gathered group was often moved to tears as Charles prayed.[50]

Reflecting on his childhood, Thomas Spurgeon said that family worship was a "delightful item of each day's doings."[51] Too often the word "delightful" is not associated with family worship—but it can, and should, be a delightful experience of encountering God in the Bible, seeking God in prayer, and singing hymns.

In Victorian England, the family was regarded as vital to cultural prosperity. Historian Walter E. Houghton described the Victorian family: "Its ritual is well known: the gathering of the whole household for family prayers, the attendance together at church on Sunday morning, the reading aloud in the evenings, the family vacation."[52] For Charles and Susie, family worship was no mere cultural tradition; it was one way they fulfilled the biblical mandate of Psalm 78:4 to tell their children "the praises of the LORD, and his strength, and his wonderful works that he hath done." That said, when they gathered with all members of their household, children, servants, and guests, they were joining with many other Englanders who were also engaging in family devotional exercises.

Charles and Susie couldn't have skillfully navigated life together apart from individual and family worship. Reading Scripture was like food for their souls, meditation was like crushing grapes for the best wine, prayer was entering into the welcoming arms of their heavenly Father to praise Him and to embrace His promises, and family worship was simply what godly families did, for God is worthy of worship. Such times were rich in instruction for both Charles and Susie and their household. When Charles wrote his devotional book *Morning by Morning*, he had a vision of sharing in "hallowed communion with thousands of families all over the world, every morning at the family altar."[53]

Whether reading the Bible and praying privately or engaging in family worship, Charles and Susie were not half-hearted in their efforts. Susie encouraged readers of her books not to be content with a "sickly, spiritual life as such dishonors Christ and hurts oneself."[54] Charles and Susie simply kept "drinking of that [the Bible] living water constantly," and they were "refreshed and strengthened thereby for suffering or for service."[55]

Biographer Russell Conwell points to Charles and Susie's "cheerful trust in God, unshakable love for each other, and a domestic peace such as only the most perfect English homes enjoy."[56] Though Charles and Susie are a stellar example of marital love, they would not have imagined their home as "perfect." However, their home was characterized by the peace of God and they were enabled by their spirituality for their shared mission.

CHAPTER 3

Shared Mission

GODLY WOMEN WERE INSTRUMENTAL in the making of Charles Spurgeon. There was his mother who had so often urged him to repent in his youth; his grandmother who was known for her piety; his aunt Ann who attended to him during his childhood; and Mary King, the cook from Newmarket, whom he credited with his Calvinistic theology. These were all women he loved and admired. But Susie towered above them all in his affections; she was his friend, his confidant, his lover, and his most ardent defender. She was wise about the city in which they ministered, and she wholeheartedly embraced, gave her life to, and shared his mission.

Susie was smart and humble, evidenced by her receiving and seeking Charles's counsel when facing a dilemma. She was strong—not crushed beneath the burdens they bore, and she fully supported Charles. She believed in him, so teamwork was not only a necessity, it was a delight.

Conwell said of Susie, "She could curb the uncouth eccentricities and correct his mistakes in language or history, and she hesitated not in the most affectionate manner to apply her criticisms where she saw they would do her husband good."[1] Charles welcomed Susie's opinions and counsel. He had undertaken a tremendous responsibility in accepting a prominent London pastorate at such a young age and with limited experience. Susie was knowledgeable about the ways of London and she was acquainted with the New Park Street Chapel and its traditions. Charles needed Susie.[2]

Charles married a woman who "worked with him, prayed with him, believed in him, and most affectionately loved him through those many years of his work."[3] Perhaps this is in part what Charles meant when he intimated that Susie was necessary to him: he had work to do, and he needed a wife at his side who prioritized his vision.

A part of that vision was church planting. It is estimated that Charles planted two hundred churches across the Continent, and that during his ministry, the number of churches reflecting his theology doubled.[4] Spurgeon's ministry transformed England, in large part, through those mission churches that dotted the landscape— many of them staffed by students from his college. Susie's love, support, and unheralded sacrifice were essential to the realization of this vision.

Susie's temperament, in at least one important way, was vital for Charles's ministry to function healthily. Charles was prone to seasons of melancholy while Susie was not, though she was sometimes plagued by anxiety. Her commitment to his ministry, evidenced by her vow to never hinder him in his work nor expect him to be present even in her sicknesses, freed him to become the man who shook the world in his day and the preacher we still admire today. Susie's value to Charles is difficult to measure, but it was immense. Had she not willingly and lovingly sacrificed for his mission and ministry, the story of Charles Spurgeon would be different and, perhaps, just a footnote in church history.

SUSIE'S LOVING SACRIFICES

In 1875, the Baptist Union held its fall meeting at Plymouth. Spurgeon preached a sermon on October 5 in which he honored faithful Christians who had died during the year. He lamented the loss of friends and associates, but he envisioned in their deaths a motivation to even more active service, especially evangelism. During that meeting, Charles's "domestic trials were of a most distressing kind." As he spoke of the death of comrades in ministry, his mind was on Susie, who was herself teetering on the precipice between life and death back at home.

A pastor reported: "In coming to Plymouth [Charles] had left behind him in London a dearly-loved but greatly-suffering wife, whose long-continued and most painful affliction would have caused deep sorrow and anxiety to an even less affectionate husband than he who had just spoken." Susie's "condition was now eminently critical, but from her dying bed she had that day telegraphed to her husband not to return home, but to go forward with his work at Plymouth." Though Charles was anxious, he remained; Susie took a decidedly positive turn for the better, and God spared her life and Charles further grief.[5]

It is fair to think that Charles should have returned home, regardless of Susie's request. From our side of history, it is hard to imagine a scenario where a loving husband would not move heaven and earth to get to his dying wife. But lest we be too hard on Charles, it is always difficult to make judgments on such decisions of folks who lived long ago. So, though we scratch our heads over Charles's choice, we can use it to think through what our responses should be if we found ourselves in a similar situation. It is also reasonable to conclude that Susie's commitment not to hinder Charles in his work certainly did not extend to her deathbed. But Susie found her joy in embracing Charles's calling to the fullest extent possible, even foregoing his presence in her hour of need. Her numerous loving sacrifices were designed to cheer him in his work. She wanted him to feel free to serve without worrying about whether she was suffering. Though she missed him, she didn't grumble. Otherwise, he could not have functioned as energetically as he did.

Susie's Heart and Soul Support

Early in their marriage, Susie supported Charles's ministry by counseling and assisting female baptismal candidates at church. Her influence was significant, as the women testified to even after Susie's death, and Charles was helped by Susie attending to the spiritual well-being of women who were new converts. After Susie died, Thomas Spurgeon reported: "How many greet me, to this day, with such glad words as these, 'She led me to the baptismal pool, you know, and I shall never forget her loving words to me.'"[6]

Susie labored to undergird and to extend her husband's ministry in every way she could; she supported translating his sermons into foreign languages, getting his books into the hands of needy pastors, assisting him at the Pastors' College and the orphanages, and opening their home as a haven of hospitality to students, church leaders, and travelers. Such hospitality endeared the hearts of many to the couple, including the famous American evangelist D. L. Moody and his wife, Emma. The Moodys became close friends of Charles and Susie, and, whenever the Moodys visited London, they ministered and socialized together.

One of Charles's early biographers wrote of Susie's "quiet, unobtrusive way in which it [her work] is conducted," and he honored her for her lovely Christian demeanor and devotion to serving others.[7] Susie exemplified such humble service in various ministry pursuits, all of which bolstered Charles's work. Her first biographer, Charles Ray, wrote in 1903, "In every branch of his work, she threw her heart and soul ... it would be difficult to find anywhere another woman, who in spite of adverse circumstances ... did such monumental work for God and man."[8]

Susie was Charles's true partner in service. Absorbed in his life and work, she had no expressed independent personal ambitions. His interests were her interests. Though she is now remembered for her many accomplishments, she never even thought of herself apart from Charles. She delighted in his company, was proud of his accomplishments, and kept a detailed record of his ministry by collecting news clippings and articles into scrapbooks, some of which are still available today in the archives at Spurgeon's College in London.

None of this should imply that Susie was not affected by the challenges of being married to a famous preacher. She sometimes paced the floor awaiting Charles's return home at night, breathing a sigh of relief when his footsteps were heard approaching the door. She struggled with fear of being alone and worried about her overworked husband. On one occasion, she wept as Charles departed for yet another trip out of town. Charles looked into Susie's eyes and said, "You are giving me to God in letting me go to preach the Gospel to poor sinners."[9]

He compared her sacrifice to the ancient Israelite who offered up his sacrificial lamb and left it at the altar, not to be reclaimed.

Tenderly, Charles commended Susie's sacrificial commitment. Perhaps, as much as anything else, she shared his gospel mission by encouraging him.

> My beloved husband, always so engaged about his
> Master's business, yet managed to secure many precious
> moments by my side; when he would tell me how the
> work of the Lord was prospering in his hands, and we
> would exchange sympathies, he comforting me in my
> suffering, and I cheering him on in his labor.[10]

Charles was a joyful recipient of Susie's "cheering" support, *and* he stood with her in all of her various pursuits. He served as editor for her writing endeavors (though he felt her writing was perfect on its own), a benefactor to her Book Fund, a ready counselor when she found herself in sticky situations, and as one who was constantly challenging her to a life of service. The March 1892 edition of *The Ladies Home Journal* included a biographical sketch of Susie:

> She became president of various societies having, in
> some form or other, the people's good as their object. She
> visited the sick among her husband's rapidly increasing
> congregation. She founded the Working Missionary
> Society among the women who from far and near attend
> the Tabernacle. She formed the Pastors' Aid Society by
> means of which poor parsons, their wives and children,
> are furnished with warm winter clothing.[11]

Charles and Susie's mutual endeavors were founded on shared convictions, especially regarding the fundamentals of the faith; such was necessary for their marriage to thrive. They didn't always agree on all secondary or tertiary matters. For example, Charles was opposed to musical accompaniment in congregational singing.

However, later in life, Susie gave organs to at least two churches to aid in their congregational worship, one of them a church Charles had started and another that she planted as a memorial to him. To the first one, Susie wrote in July of 1888 that she had learned of their desire to purchase a musical instrument to "secure better congregational singing." She stipulated that her gift of an American organ was contingent on the church only using it for worship and never for entertainment. She presented the organ as an offering of thanksgiving to God for sustaining her through another illness and as an appreciation to the church for their prayers for her.[12]

Though Charles used bazaars to raise money for the Metropolitan Tabernacle, Susie later opposed them, writing a provocative treatise, *A Protest Against Bazaars* (1896). It may be that Susie's view in 1896 reflected a change on her part, or perhaps Charles embraced Susie's perspective before he died. She urged churches *not* to employ bazaars or any other secular activities to financially support their ministries.[13]

Their differences of opinion fostered no division between them, though it is likely they enjoyed a few lively conversations.

The first ten years of their marriage provided the greatest opportunities for Charles and Susie to minister together. Charles often traveled without Susie, as she had a busy home to manage, twin sons to raise, and a team of household staff to oversee. In addition, she managed her small dairy farm and flower ministry from home. However, there were numerous occasions when they worked side by side and traveled the Continent together. Some of their travels were for pleasure: touring historic sites, perusing art galleries, viewing the valleys below from high in the Alps, and simply enjoying one another's company. That said, Charles's journeys always included ministry activities. He was frequently asked to preach, and he traveled with books, paper, and pen so that he could work on writing projects in his spare minutes. Susie supported all.

Charles and Susie's joint efforts were especially directed to society's downtrodden—widows, orphans, and the families of poor pastors. One of the lesser-known works that Susie presided over was a ministry to destitute mothers. The Metropolitan Maternal Society provided staple items to help sustain impoverished mothers and their children.[14] For the Spurgeons, true religion fostered gospel-driven social action. Charles exhorted his church members that every single one of them ought to be involved in assisting his fellow man.[15]

Mike Nicholls, in *The Pastor Evangelist*, analyzed Spurgeon's commitment as a Christian activist:

> Spurgeon was not a social reformer in the generally accepted sense, his primary task was to preach the gospel, but he was not indifferent or insensitive to the everyday needs of the poor. . . .
>
> [He] was a big man, with a big heart, and this found expression in many acts of charity. No one contended more strongly than Spurgeon that the gospel was not a social gospel, but a redeeming gospel. That redeeming gospel, however, carries social implications, which for Spurgeon meant the Stockwell Orphanage, the Ragged School, and the homes for old people [that he founded or lead].[16]

Charles's concern for the needy led biographer J. C. Carlile to compare him to Charles Dickens, whose books helped create awareness of the plight that the lower classes of the Victorian era faced. "Dickens in his crowded pages gave special care to 'the thousand and one next to nothings' that make up the life of the common people. It was so with Spurgeon."[17]

Great literature again provides a fitting analogy. Playing off of *The Pilgrim's Progress*, Susie characterized her marriage to Charles as pilgrims on a journey together.[18] Grounded on theological convictions, focused on Christ and His gospel, and invested in loving others, Charles and Susie enjoyed a unity of heart and a common commitment to ministry.

THE GOVERNOR AND THE MOTHER

Charles was a man of ambitious vision who pressed forward with confident faith in God's provision. He admitted that sometimes Susie didn't understand his varied pursuits, yet she trusted him, and she shared his Christ-centered objectives. A driving passion of Charles's was to invest in men who felt called to ministry and to provide them with a basic and practical theological/ministerial education. Shortly after he and Susie returned from their Paris honeymoon in January of 1856, he took on his first student.

The sort of students that captured Charles's attention were men of modest means who couldn't afford a traditional college. Beyond the cost, however, lay Charles's concern that pastors would not be well-served in many of the existing colleges and, in some cases, have their faith undermined. Financial *and* theological issues were motivating factors in his formation of the Pastors' College—and this ministry was closest to his heart. By the time he died in 1892, Spurgeon had trained almost a thousand pastors, helping hundreds of them to secure places of ministry.

The growth of the college resulted in a wider footprint for Spurgeon as a network sprung up that was comprised of his own former students. Spurgeon was revered by most of the men he trained; they saw him as a father figure. This magnified Spurgeon's pain when, later in his ministry, some of those men abandoned him.

The Pastors' College was called "a romance of faith."[19] To be successful, a few practical matters needed to be considered, not the least of which was money. Such a significant enterprise as the college affected not only Charles but also Susie. Success for the college required Susie to open their home to students and to trim the family budget. Since the college's earliest financial support came from Charles and Susie's own funds, sacrifices were made by Susie to an already slender budget.[20]

It was from a "small beginning" with one student, T. W. Medhurst, a relatively new convert and a rope maker, that the Pastors' College was established.[21] Spurgeon's friend William Williams remembered,

> The Pastors' College was the first philanthropic
> institution that Mr. Spurgeon founded, and to the last it
> was dearer to his heart than any other. To no other work
> did he give himself with more absolute consecration of
> money and mind and heart than to the training of his
> men for the Christian ministry; and in the judgment of
> not a few of the ministers educated in the College, the
> splendor of his ability and the greatness of his character
> were more conspicuous as President than either as author
> or preacher.[22]

Charles and Susie were never seriously threatened by poverty, even though their finances occasionally dangled near the edge. Susie recalled that there were times that "the coffers of both College and household were well-nigh empty."[23] If Susie had not shared her husband's faith and vision of training pastors, and if she had been unwilling to trim expenditures, the added stress on their marriage might have undone them.

On a particular occasion, funds were especially low, and Charles asked, "Wifey, what can we do?"[24] The enterprising pastor considered giving up his hired horse that carried him to church services, but Susie protested that his transportation was a necessity and not a luxury. She would look for other ways to cut expenses, but she could not bear the thought of her husband's pain being multiplied by the loss of his horse. She recalled, "Long and anxiously we pondered over ways and means, and laid our burden before the Lord, entreating Him to come to our aid. And, of course, He heard and answered, for He is a faithful God."[25] Within a day or two, they received an anonymous letter with £20 inside. Though the identity of the benefactor was never revealed, both Charles and Susie recognized that God had heard their prayers and provided for their needs. Charles kept his horse and the college maintained its support.

Susie loved that Charles was in his element with the students. At the college, he spun humor freely, and his ability to have fun was obvious to all. One writer declared, "In the presence of his students he seemed to be as much at home and as free from all restraints as in the quiet seclusion of his own home."[26] Most importantly, "Spurgeon's Men" were trained in essential doctrine and the nuts-and-bolts of pastoral ministry, and encouraged to a life of practical holiness.

Susie was affectionately called the "Mother of the College" while Charles was called the "Governor." When students gathered at the Spurgeon home on Saturdays, Susie enjoyed entertaining them—and watching Charles interact with them. She was a gracious, encouraging, and motherly host. She also provided thousands of excellent books over the course of her lifetime to students and alumni, choosing titles designed to help them in their ministries.

TOGETHER IN ALL THINGS SMALL AND LARGE

Unity of mission and purpose was at the heart of Charles and Susie's joyful marriage. Charles proclaimed, no doubt with Susie in mind, that a "model marriage" was one of love and esteem. In such a marriage, the husband is "a tender head" and the wife "delights in her husband" and considers him "the chief and foremost of mankind" and her "all-in-all." Her love is for him and him alone. She is content, comforted, and joyful in his company, and she is honored in her husband's honor.[27] Charles was not a domineering husband nor was Susie a reluctant wife—they found freedom and joy in their roles and by pulling together, they accomplished great things for God's glory.

It was imperative that Charles and Susie were in solidarity regarding family and ministry. After all, they had twin boys within the first year of their marriage, a growing church, and demands of time and energy related to Spurgeon's unique popularity. They knew that a successful marriage meant mutual commitment and shared priorities. Charles said of such a husband and wife that they share a common objective in life and that they often think the same thoughts at the same time.[28]

According to Charles, the happiest of couples are those who "are so blended, so engrafted on one stem, that their old age presents a lovely attachment, a common sympathy, by which its infirmities are greatly alleviated, and its burdens are transformed into fresh bonds of love." He mused: "So happy a union of will, sentiment, thought, and heart exists between them, that the two streams of their lives have washed away the dividing bank, and run on as one broad current of united existence till their common joy falls into the ocean of eternal felicity."[29]

THE PLOUGHMAN AND THE ANGEL

"John Ploughman" was Charles's pseudonym for a series of articles in *The Sword and the Trowel*, and later "John" found his way into a couple of Charles's books about a wise country farmer who dispensed wisdom on subjects near and far. The two books, *John Ploughman's Talk* and *John Ploughman's Pictures*, contain moral maxims and cover topics ranging from debt to the dangers of alcohol to marriage and family. The volumes sold over half a million copies during Charles's and Susie's lifetimes and are still published today. John Ploughman said, "Show me a loving husband, a worthy wife, and good children and no pair of horses that ever flew along the road could take me in a year where I could see a more pleasing sight."[30]

"John" called home "the grandest of institutions." Writing of the "rubbish" that some men expressed about their wives, Charles said that such slander "does not prove that the women are bad, but that their husbands are good for nothing." Acknowledging that there were some "shockingly bad wives in the world," he countered, "Take them for all in all, they are most angelic creatures, and a great deal too good for half the husbands."[31] "Angel" was one of Charles's favorite nouns for Susie.

As Charles mused about these "angelic" creatures, it is clear that his reference is to his own sweet Susie. "A true wife is her husband's better half, his lump of delight [sweet candy], his flower of beauty, his guardian angel, and his heart's treasure." Charles found in Susie a slice of heaven on earth, as she brightened his life and comforted his soul. Susie was Charles's "rib . . . the best bone in his body."[32] Spurgeon may have been profuse in his metaphors, using both biblical and humorous descriptors, but perhaps such language was closer to the Song of Solomon—one of Spurgeon's favorite books of the Bible—than to Spurgeon's own Victorian culture.

Despite his robust and overt affection toward his wife, Charles was so intensely focused on ministry that he was sometimes inattentive toward Susie. She noticed this first during their engagement and, on at least one occasion, she was deeply hurt. Amends were made, the relationship thrived, and later Charles's distractedness became fodder for joking around. Soon after their reconciliation, and still early in their engagement, Charles mailed an invitation for Susie to join him on a preaching trip to Windsor. He wrote, "Possibly, I may be again inattentive to you if you do go; but this will be nice for us both,—that 'Charles' may have space for mending, and that 'Susie' may exhibit her growth in knowledge of his character, by patiently enduring his failings." For Susie, "the end of this little 'rift in the lute' was no patched-up peace, instead, the deepening of our confidence in each other, and an increase of that fervent love which can look at a misunderstanding in the face till it melts away and vanishes, as a morning cloud before the ardent glances of the sun."[33]

Charles recognized that his intensity for his public ministry was sometimes difficult for Susie, and he didn't take his failures lightly. He cared deeply about Susie's feelings and expressed that no one knew how grateful to God he was for her—grateful because she loved and served God devotedly, she delighted in his happiness, and her positive attitude made him better able to minister. He wrote to Susie that her friendship and support had enabled him to serve God more faithfully: "I have served the Lord far more, and never less, for your sweet companionship."[34]

Charles, like any sensitive husband, felt guilty at times for his absence from home. His unceasing work often squeezed out opportunities for him to pay adequate attention due to Susie. Her sacrificial service on his behalf did not go unnoticed by him. He asserted, "No woman has ever more readily entered into all her husband's plans for the extension of the Redeemer's kingdom, nor more readily spared him from her side when called away upon 'the King's business.'"[35]

Susie referred to Charles as her "precious husband" and her "life's beloved."[36] She considered his voice as "the sweetest in all the world to me."[37] Susie was "doubly dear" to Charles,[38] his "wifey," "my own darling," and "my own dear one."[39]

Charles "delighted in paying tribute to the angel of his house" (a popular phrase in Victorian times that idealized women). But for Charles, the phrase indicated how highly he regarded Susie.[40] Biographer Earnest Bacon wrote, "God had certainly made them for each other. It was a love match, but also a spiritual partnership, as every true Christian marriage should be. Heavily did they lean upon each other. Closely were their hearts and aims intertwined. Richly did the Lord bless and use them together."[41]

Their work was indeed shared, so much so that when Susie referred to the monthly missive started in 1865 by Charles, *The Sword and the Trowel*, she referred to it as "our magazine."[42] This was more than a spirit of collaboration. Charles depended on Susie's feedback, input, and her pen; her contributions eventually led to her own endeavors as an author.

SHEPHERDING GOD'S SHEPHERDS

In 1875, Spurgeon's first volume of *Lectures to My Students* was released. Just prior, he gave Susie a proof copy to read. Susie excitedly told him that she wanted every pastor in England to read his book. She was a bit taken aback, however, when Charles challenged her to lead such an effort. Hesitatingly, she accepted his challenge, which resulted in Mrs. Spurgeon's Book Fund, a ministry of The Metropolitan Tabernacle. Ultimately, under Susie's guidance, the ministry gave away almost two hundred thousand books, many of them authored by Charles, to poor pastors.

Through the Book Fund, Susie found ways to minister, not only to pastors but also to their families through gifts of clothes, supplies, and occasionally even money. Susie's objective was to provide pastors, who otherwise couldn't afford them, doctrinally sound and gospel-centered resources that would teach pastors and stir their hearts. She believed these books would make for better preachers and stronger churches.[43]

Mrs. Spurgeon's Book Fund is familiar to Spurgeon aficionados, and its story is recounted in some detail in *Susie: The Life and Legacy of Susannah Spurgeon.* What is not as obvious is the depth of partnership between Charles and Susie in this endeavor. Susie gave her heart and soul to the mission, answering letters, writing reports, choosing books, and overseeing the mailings, and Charles vigorously encouraged the life work of his wife via prayer and financial support and by including Susie's monthly reports in each edition of *The Sword and the Trowel.*

At times, Charles insisted that Susie cease work for a season when she was overwhelmed by the responsibilities and burdened with affliction. The Book Fund ministry was important, but not as important to Charles as was the health of his beloved. At such times either Charles assisted Susie, or he would enlist one of his assistants to help her.[44]

Although Charles was delighted by Susie's literary efforts, she preferred not to submit her written reports for publication without his approval. She desired his careful editorial eye because she trusted him completely, not because she feared his displeasure.

However, she was sometimes reluctant to ask for help out of concern of taking up too much of his time. Charles explained:

> Moreover, my dear one has so poor an idea of her
> own abilities that she almost always submitted her
> compositions to my revision; and though my verdict
> upon her writing so entirely differs from her own that I
> seldom alter a word, yet she cannot bring herself to the
> task without me, nor would she lay an ounce weight of
> labour upon me by asking me to look at her pages and
> therefore it was determined that she would this year
> leave the Report to be written by a friend.[45]

Despite their much-needed times of respite, requests for books continued to pour into Susie's mailbox. Each letter had to be examined and answered. Books were chosen for qualified pastors, and they were then wrapped, packaged, and mailed. Funds and other donations were received, and they had to be accounted for. Susie was a meticulous bookkeeper, keeping a detailed diary of her efforts which, in turn, increased her work. Amazingly, she accomplished all of her Book Fund work while an invalid.

When the Fund began in 1875, Susie's affliction was a grave concern; it had been for several years. However, though managing the Fund was difficult, the work turned out to be therapeutic for Susie as it provided a godly distraction from her sufferings and helped to focus her on a great work. Charles encouraged others to learn from Susie's example to employ "self-sacrificing work for the Lord Jesus" as a means to help them to be profitable servants of God, even in the midst of suffering.[46]

Susie, through the Book Fund, rose above the walls of her house and entered the homes of thousands of needy pastors, bringing gifts that lifted their spirits and encouraged their ministries.

A warm letter Susie wrote to her "editor" demonstrates that she recognized that the Book Fund was a shared mission. She requested her "very dear Mr. Editor" if he would include in the coming month's *Sword and the Trowel* "one, clear and jubilant, and grateful blessing on behalf of the Book Fund":

> Tell the dear friends who read *The Sword and the Trowel* that "my mouth is filled with laughter, and my tongue with singing" at the remembrance of the gracious love which continues to give support, and sustenance, and success to me in my beloved work . . .
>
> Ah! Dear Mr. Editor, sound the notes of praise for me! I want God's people to know how *very* good He is to unworthy me, that they may take comfort and courage from my experience of His tenderness and love.
>
> Yours with true love and "reverence."
>
> S. Spurgeon.[47]

Charles and Susie shared a lifetime of service together. After Charles died in 1892, Susie continued *their* work as if her beloved husband were still by her side. Their shared mission is but a component of their mutual support—a support most obvious in their labors and in their sufferings.

CHAPTER 4

CHARLES SPURGEON INHERITED his grandfather's happy contentment, evident in James's fifty-year ministry and his delight in the simple sights and sounds of nature. Charles called Stambourne "my Grandfather's country."[1] He often meditated on his childhood spent at his grandfather's knee or walking beside him as they visited members of his congregation. Awed by God's mercies to him, Charles considered all of his life—from Stambourne to Colchester to London—a "fairy dream."[2] At the heart of his dreamy life was Susie.

"Fairy dream" didn't imply that Charles imagined that his ministry and marriage were easy. His upbeat language was more an acknowledgment of God's sustaining grace than idealistic circumstances. Charles and Susie's marriage and ministry *was* a fairy-dream of love, opportunity, and support *in spite of* rough waters.

They maintained a happy marriage because they stood beside one another in the midst of hardships.

Charles and Susie's marriage was bookended by two traumatic experiences: the Music Hall Disaster in the first year of their marriage and the Down-Grade Controversy near the end of Charles's life. In between were depression, physical challenges, and other issues of great concern.

Just months after establishing their first home—and only one month after the birth of their twin sons—a great shadow fell upon the Spurgeon household, one that threatened their sanity, the stability of their home life, and Charles's health and ministry.

The Music Hall Disaster was one of the pivotal events in Spurgeon's life and ministry and, though analyzed to some extent in *Susie: The Life and Legacy of Susannah Spurgeon*, it should also be considered from a fresh perspective here because of the effect that it had on Charles and Susie's marriage.

TERROR IN THE GARDENS
AND TRIUMPH IN A GARDEN

After this horrific event, during which seven people were trampled to death, Charles's depression, previously and comparatively rather mild, deepened. Susie wrote, "My beloved's anguish was so deep and violent, that reason seemed to totter in her throne, and we sometimes feared that he would never preach again."[3] Suicidal thoughts sometimes struck their wicked bolts into Charles's psyche. He lamented, "I could readily enough have laid violent hands upon myself, to escape from my misery of spirit."[4]

Why was Charles preaching at the Music Hall in the first place? With a congregation spilling out of the New Park Street

Chapel's building twice each Sunday, church leadership decided to temporarily rent larger facilities in the city while the church's sanctuary was expanded (later rebuilt in a new location and renamed the Metropolitan Tabernacle, which opened in 1861). One of the facilities chosen was the Royal Surrey Gardens Music Hall. The ornate, three-story building could seat at least ten thousand and pack in an additional two thousand.

On Sunday evening, October 19, 1856, the first night the church employed the Hall, Charles was attempting to address the huge crowd inside the facility, while an equally large crowd pressed around the building outside. A panic ensued in the packed-out hall when agitators cried "fire" and yelled that the roof was falling. Neither was true. Screams echoed throughout the great edifice; some people leapt from the balcony, others stampeded and crushed their fellow congregants. Death, injury, and heartbreak resulted. Seven people died; twenty-eight others were injured. Charles collapsed under the stress of the darkest night of his life.

Susie was at home, recovering from giving birth to twins just a few weeks prior, and quite unaware of what was happening with Charles. Her night—or rather, her *life*—was soon to be dramatically changed.

Charles later wrote that it was a night that time would never erase from his memory. "Tears were my meat by day and dreams my terror by night." Anguished, he refused to be comforted. "Here my mind lay, like a wreck upon the sand, incapable of its usual motion. I was in a strange land, and a stranger in it."[5] He struggled to read the Bible and he found no comfort in prayer. The press slandered him, accusing him of exasperating the panicked crowds and causing him to say that they "might have scooped out the last drop of consolation from my cup of happiness."[6] He considered himself the lowest of the low, dwelling in the "nethermost depths."[7]

Charles was in a "season of darkness where neither sun nor moon appeared." Even the loveliness of Jesus, normally an ever-present meditation of his mind, escaped him. There was nothing Susie could say—Charles had no ability to hear. She was deeply troubled and afraid for the health of her husband. Susie—a twenty-four-year-old new mother of twins, deeply in love with her husband of only ten months—was faced with a challenge of monumental proportion: helping to uphold her husband and to facilitate his mental stability. Yet, as Charles revealed in a letter to his mother soon after, Susie was very sick herself. Charles's spirit was broken; Susie's body felt broken—they both wondered what would happen to them.

The season seemed calamitous, but God eventually delivered Charles from his dark dungeon, though not without scars. Charles announced that God had arrested him with hope. "On a sudden, like a flash of lightning from the sky, my soul returned unto me. The burning lava of my brain cooled in an instant. The throbbings of my brow were still; the cool wind of comfort fanned my cheek which had been scorched in the furnace."[8] Now free, he "leaped for joy of heart," and was restored to his "right and happy state." He declared, "I was a man again, and what is more, a believer."[9] Had Charles doubted his salvation during this time?

Charles's renewed perspective occurred as he walked with Susie in a garden while meditating on the promises of God. Gardens were sacred to Charles: When he was a boy, a traveling missionary sat with him in his grandfather's garden and prophesied that he would preach the gospel. Charles had proposed marriage to Susie in her grandfather's garden. And now, in this lovely garden at the home of a deacon, he found peace in his trial. This garden was Eden to Charles, and for the rest of his life he considered it a holy place.

His heart overflowed with song as he praised God: he said that it was the most delightful day of contemplating the glory of God since his conversion.[10]

Though it *was* a day of restoration, Charles never fully recovered.

Susie encouraged her suffering husband by reminding him of God's promises. As she was apt to do throughout their marriage, she framed Bible verses and placed them in strategic places in their home. The walls of their home then proclaimed the goodness of God as Charles gazed upon God's guarantees. Though God restored Charles's sanity, joy, and his ability to preach again, he was, nevertheless, disfigured emotionally; and, when he returned to NPSC two weeks later, and to the Music Hall after only four weeks, to preach, his fragility was obvious to Susie.

Charles's ministry flourished after this recovery but tears more easily welled-up in his eyes when his emotions were provoked. At other times, he would sit seemingly paralyzed, gripped by the memory of that awful night—the sounds of people shrieking and sights of the panicked crowd entering his mind as unwelcomed guests. Still other times, he had to brace himself against a beam or some other stable object prior to entering the pulpit due to nervousness.

The consequences of the disaster were experienced not by Spurgeon alone; they were also felt in his home, in the pulpit, and by his beloved Susie. William Williams, one of Charles's closest comrades, reflected on the effects of that horrific episode on his friend and concluded that the depth of his mental suffering was partly responsible for his early death.[11] If not the cause of his death, it certainly contributed. Added to his other multiplied sorrows, by the time he was fifty-seven, the effects became too much for his body or mind to bear.

What would have become of Charles without Susie by his side?

It's an unanswerable question—at least definitively. However, her personal stability, prayerfulness, and companionship were certainly encouraging to him. Under the crushing trials that plagued Charles, Susie might have unraveled. However, "she bore up and by her words of comfort, her strong affection, and her piety and faith, [she] helped him to weather the gale."[12] It is likely that Susie was the human means that God used not only to rescue Charles's ministry but also to save his life. Charles said as much: "My wife's presence is also a main ingredient in my cup, which runs over with mercies."[13]

WALKING TOGETHER THROUGH THE DUNGEON OF DEPRESSION

Depression frequently assailed Charles before the Music Hall tragedy—but afterwards, his despondency deepened. During a Friday lecture at the Pastors' College, Spurgeon commented to his students, "One crushing stroke has sometimes laid the minister very low."[14] He spoke with surprising vulnerability of his excruciating experiences with depression. Charles's intent was not to elicit pity, but to offer comfort to his students. He wanted them to know that such trials, though unwelcomed at the time, were common and even useful. He shared honestly so that "younger men might not fancy that some strange thing had happened to them when they became for a season possessed by melancholy; and that sadder men might know that one upon whom the sun has shone right joyously did not always walk in the light."[15]

Charles didn't see himself as a helpless victim; instead, he chose to press into Christ via prayer and ministry when he traversed dark valleys. And Susie walked deep into those valleys with him—as far as she could descend while keeping her own footing.

Charles needed Susie's aid when he was submerged in sadness. He recalled, "My spirits were sunken so low that I could weep by the hour like a child, and yet I know not what I wept for."[16] Imagine Susie finding her husband crying uncontrollably and without explanation. She threw her arms around him and held him closely as he sobbed. Feeling her near him was comforting. She buttressed him through all sorts of trials and, in fact, made him a better man.[17]

In his suffering, Charles felt God's hand drawing him near to his Savior. He asserted, "When they [suffering and pain] bring men as near to Jesus as they carried us, they are not angels in disguise, but seraphs all unveiled."[18] He also recognized that his suffering was not his alone. His marriage was "a spiritual partnership."[19] When either Charles or Susie was laid low, the other fought back against encroaching darkness by looking heavenward for light.

Spurgeon biographer H. I. Wayland surmised that Susie was the reason Charles was able to go "through his unparalleled labors" and that she facilitated "rest and refreshment" for him at home. She provided "the society of a brave, noble, [and] loving woman."[20] Susie's conviction of the total sovereignty of God buttressed her; and through her, it strengthened Charles. Susie's confession of faith in such hard times is summed up in her words: "In times of trouble the soul is greatly helped by cherishing great thoughts of God."[21]

Employing Bunyan's language, Susie recognized that though she and Charles, and all Christians, might be "a company of Feeble-minds, and Much-afraids, and Fearings, and Ready-to-halts," they should not delay in seeking God in prayer. She believed that though Christians might be weak in faith, depressed in heart, and jaded in mind, there is a gracious, loving, and merciful God ready not only to hear their humble cries but grant them the desires of their heart.[22] She rested her expectation on the promise of Isaiah 41:10: "I will strengthen thee; yea, I will help thee." What a wife and friend that Charles had in Susie—no wonder he so often sang her praises.

Charles's faith was cut of the same cloth as Susie's. He considered God's promises, set in their biblical context, as certainties.

> A promise from God may very instructively be compared to a cheque payable to order. It is given to the believer with the view of bestowing upon him some good thing. It is not meant that he should read it over comfortably, and then have done with it. No, he is to treat the promise as a reality, as a man treats a cheque.[23]

God intends to give His good gifts of grace to His children; Charles *and* Susie were recipients of those good gifts.

In the midst of their fiery troubles, the Spurgeons experienced the goodness of God more practically. Charles declared, "My brethren, God is good. He will not forsake you; He will bear you through." He further testified, "He has been to me so faithful in countless instances that I must encourage you to trust Him."[24] This is one reason that common men and women heard Charles so gladly; his message was embodied in his life—a life that he shared honestly with his congregation.

Such faith in the promises of God and such love and support from Susie helped Charles to hang on and to move forward when the black dog of depression howled at him at midnight.[25] Spurgeon considered depression the worst of his sufferings, for it usually carried with it a sense of the loss of God's presence, something he feared most.[26] "Let a man be abandoned to despair, and he is ready for all sorts of sins. When fear unnerves him, action is dangerous; but when despair has loosed his joints and paralyzed his conscience, the vultures hover round him waiting for their prey."[27] The vultures hovered over Charles during many a dark night.

Though it cannot be determined with certainty the most prominent agency of Spurgeon's depression, it likely was a combination of several issues: (1) his overall poor physical health, (2) the pressures of his various trials (theological controversy, a sick wife, and overwhelming ministry responsibilities), (3) his personality (Spurgeon believed that some people are more prone to depression than are others), and (4) something akin to post-traumatic stress disorder (PTSD),[28] especially following the Music Hall Disaster and Down-Grade Controversy.

Biographer Richard Day surmised that Spurgeon's grief over the Music Hall Disaster nearly "unseated his reason. He was immediately hidden from the public; spent hours in tears by day, and dreams of terror by night. A depression complex deepened upon him from which he never fully recovered."[29]

Charles described depression as "dungeons beneath the Castle of Despair as dreary as the abodes of the lost."[30] And even with Susie near to him, he was sometimes distressed. He regretted his depressions, saying, "They render me very bad company."[31] Susie was the recipient of his "bad company" and it saddened her—not because she was inconvenienced, but because she was grieved to see the one she dearly loved so oppressed by sadness. And, though Charles was bad company and couldn't sleep during some of those times, he admitted he needed someone to talk to.

Though he suffered with depression, Charles's overall demeanor was one of thankfulness and cheerfulness, and he was never one to pass up the right opportunity for a humorous comment. It's not hard to imagine him turning to Susie at breakfast and saying, "There are difficulties in everything except eating pancakes."[32] God's promises, prayer, humor, and a supportive wife were all means that God used to pull Charles up when he was down and, therefore, his sadness of heart did not characterize him.

Conwell wrote that when Charles faced trials of various sorts, "there was always one who stood like a shield between him and the arrows of wickedness, quenching their fiery darts most easily with the shield of domestic love."[33] Susie made their home a house of God where her husband found rest from his troubles. "A home should be a Bethel," Charles once said. "If I had no home, the world would be like a great prison to me."[34]

MUTUAL CARE DURING PHYSICAL AFFLICTION

From late 1867, Susie's health deteriorated to the point where she rarely left home. This proved burdensome to Charles and to her as they so enjoyed one another's company and could hardly bear the thought of further separations. Her affliction, gynecological in nature, required surgery by 1869. However, little improvement came from the procedure, and she was not only confined to home but sometimes also to her bed for much of the following twenty years. Susie's affliction weighed heavily on Charles's heart.

At about the same time, Charles's own health worsened. Gout, an inflammation of the joints, was a frequent nemesis and wracked his body with pain. When asked by a friend what gout was like, Charles explained: "If you put your hand into a vice and let a man press as hard as he can, that is rheumatism; and if he can be got to press a little harder, that is gout."[35]

Spurgeon's first clearly documented case of gout, a condition from which his father also suffered, was in 1869. Likely, he was suffering from it much earlier. There were times when gout flung him into bed for lengthy periods. During one of those episodes, he prayed:

Thou art my Father, and I am thy child; and thou, as a
Father, art tender and full of mercy. I could not bear to
see my child suffer as thou makest me suffer, and if I saw
him tormented as I am now, I would do what I could to
help him, and put my arms under him to sustain him.
Wilt thou hide thy face from me, my Father? Wilt thou
still lay on a heavy hand, and not give me a smile from
thy countenance?[36]

Charles's prayer was raw with honesty—and, oddly refreshing and relatable to all who labor beneath the burdens of physical
affliction. In Charles's case, physiological maladies were numerous
and stretched his faith to its limits. God was his Father, and he
needed and expected that God would come to his aid. At times he
wondered why the delay.

Along with gout, Charles suffered kidney ailments in his early
twenties that eventually developed into Bright's disease—a chronic
inflammation of the kidneys. Mark Hopkins writes, "Nothing did
more to amplify the cycle of ecstasy and despondency than the ill-
health that dogged him for most of his ministry."[37]

J. W. Harrald, nicknamed the "Armor-Bearer," was one of
Spurgeon's personal secretaries and dearest friends. He estimated
that from the age of thirty-five (1869), Spurgeon was absent one-
third of the time from the pulpit due to pain, illness, or recuperation.[38] In October of 1869, Charles even suffered a mild case of
smallpox.[39]

The troubles that pressed down heavily upon Charles altered his
physical appearance. One woman described him as "course-looking
even to grossness, heavy in form and features." Some estimates have
Charles at well over three hundred pounds later in his life. That
said, he still was attractive in his person, for "as soon as he spoke,

one felt the same power was there and that the man himself was unchanged."[40] Another woman described him in a more favorable light, referring to "the square forehead and magnificent dark eyes redeeming it from ugliness, and every line on his face and figure speaking of power."[41] Even with Charles's rather odd appearance (short legs, large head, pale skin), many women were intrigued by him, some even searching for strands of his hair for a keepsake. In 1855, before most of his physical ailments, he wrote his mother that lockets containing his miniature were being sold in local shops.[42] Spurgeon sought no such attention as his heart was bound to one woman—and one woman only.

Because Charles had numerous stresses to his mind and body, he eventually appeared older than he was—and these stresses etched themselves deeply upon his face. As Susie looked into the eyes of the man she so dearly loved, it is easy to understand why she was concerned about him.

When Susie first met Charles, he looked like a boy, and her appearance was youthful, slim, and lovely. American biographer Richard Day, albeit prone to flowery prose, created this image of Susie: "She was slight of stature, her oval face framed in long chestnut curls . . . Sensitive tapering fingers; the adorable little grace of marked luster coming into her hazel eyes when interest was challenged." Day, citing no reference, has Susie at a "dainty five foot three!"[43] Photographs of Susie are as unique as her marriage. Some pictures of Susie are stunningly beautiful while others seem to betray the pain she felt and the affliction she suffered. Remarkably, one of the loveliest photographs of Susie was taken when she was older and had experienced some measure of renewed strength.

During her youth and early marriage, Susie could walk for miles almost effortlessly. Yet, her later physical affliction was so debilitating that exercise was out of the question and her body bore signs of the pain and inactivity. However, later in life, she regained some of her former vitality. Through all of her physiological changes, Susie remained lovely of heart; her deep faith, warm personality, and elegant demeanor made her a powerful presence even in her pain.

Sometimes Susie had difficulty praying, so distracted was she by her suffering.[44] On one particularly gloomy day, she questioned why God had not come to her aid. Reclining on her couch she sensed that the day's darkness seemed to have entered into her soul and "obscured its spiritual vision." Mentally, she struggled to understand what God was doing in the midst of her intense suffering.

"In sorrow of heart I asked, 'Why does my Lord thus deal with His child? Why does He so often send sharp and bitter pain to visit me? Why does He permit lingering weakness to hinder the sweet service I long to render His poor servants?'"[45]

The room was silent.

Then, finally, the quiet was broken by the crackling of a log burning in the fireplace.

Suddenly, she heard "a sweet soft sound, a little, clear, musical note, like the tender trill of a robin."

"'What *can* that be?'" she asked her friend and assistant, Elizabeth Thorne,[46] who was keeping her company. "'Surely no bird can be singing out there at this time of the year and night!'"

They listened and heard the "faint plaintive notes, so sweet, so melodious, yet mysterious enough to provoke for a moment [their] undisguised wonder." Elizabeth pointed out to Susie that the sound was coming from the log on the fire. Amazingly, "*the fire was letting loose the imprisoned music from the old oak's inmost heart!*"[47]

Susie discerned a message in the old, hardened oak log. She imagined that in its earlier days, it had gathered up a song from the birds that perched upon it. However, as it grew old, the song was bound up within the knots and beneath the scars acquired throughout its years, and the song of its youth was hidden away "until the fierce tongues of the flames came to consume its callousness and the vehement heat of the fire wrung from him at once a song and a sacrifice." She concluded, "Ah! Thought I, when the fire of affliction draws songs of praise from us, then, indeed, are we purified, and our God is glorified!"

Susie knew what God wanted from her *and* Charles—to allow their pain to press out a song of faith and thanksgiving.[48] Both Charles and Susie agreed that sickness was worthwhile because it taught them greater dependence on God. Susie said that her weakness caused her to be strengthened by Christ.[49] Charles viewed sickness as the best theological education that a person could receive.[50]

THE DOWN-GRADE CONTROVERSY

Early in their marriage, Susie sat amidst thousands of others each week as Charles preached. Yet, she was the only person who intuitively knew when he was suffering. If his throat was hurting, his last resort was to reach for the chili vinegar nearby, "a draught of which appeared to give a fresh force to the throat whenever it grew weary and the voice appeared likely to break down."[51] After a service she could not get to Charles to offer him comfort as lines of folks awaited a word with their pastor or a visitor from America anticipated greeting him. So, though she had a sense of his sufferings—evident in his walk or voice in the pulpit, there was little that she could do to help.

Susie loved Charles more than anyone, yet at church, she was just one more congregant, helpless to rush to her husband's aid.

However, she supported him in prayer while he was preaching and in all the ways that she could when he was at home. He felt her support during the last great trauma of his life, the Down-Grade Controversy. The crux of this controversy occurred between 1887 and 1888; however, its twisted arms reached all the way to the end of his life—Susie believed those arms pushed him over the edge.

The Down-Grade Controversy[52] was the second bookend of Charles's suffering. At its heart, the controversy was a fight for truth against encroaching liberalism. David Bebbington writes, "The pendulum was swinging away from precise doctrine and towards accommodating sensibility, even among Evangelicals."[53] Though the battle encompassed the larger evangelical community, it became centered on what Charles claimed was theological slippage in the Baptist Union, as some men did not hold to the old faith.

The problem, in part, was that the Union had no real means to keep heresy out, as it lacked a robust confession of faith to serve as a guard-rail against error; few men wanted such a confession. The lack of a descriptive and precise confessional statement worked fine when all were in general agreement as to the fundamentals of the faith and Baptist distinctives; but, as history often demonstrates, good will and union around truth at the beginning of an enterprise are no barrier to corruption later.

Charles's magazine, *The Sword and the Trowel,* sounded the alarm over theological errors, and Spurgeon himself both wrote and spoke forcefully on the issue. His warnings went unheeded, resulting in his resignation from the Union on October 28, 1887.

Charles held staunchly to the theology of Augustine, Calvin, and the Puritans; and he believed that the outworking of the "Romantic spirit of the age" would wrest the gospel from the pulpit.[54] His battle was also waged against preachers imbibing "modern culture, intellectual preaching, and aesthetic taste," thereby watering down the pulpit and weakening the faith of congregants.[55] The theological concerns that Charles had were significant. For example, there was growing acceptance of future probation—the theory that there is opportunity, after death, to trust in Christ. Such teaching was not orthodox but was part of the New Theology that threatened churches from various perspectives.

When Spurgeon alerted his readers, he was dismissed by some in the Baptist Union as a sort of grumpy old man lacking the mental prowess and emotional stability he once possessed. Most of the Union men had no stomach for controversy; they were well content with business as usual. Some considered that Charles's suffering diminished his usual clear-thinking, rendering him unable to rightly evaluate theological controversy. Others imagined that he had overreacted and had misjudged what was really happening in the Baptist Union. Charles, sharp as ever, saw the battle as nothing less than contending for the truth. He declared:

> A Christian minister must expect to lose his repute
> among men; he must be willing to suffer every reproach
> for Christ's sake; but, then, he may rest assured that he
> will never lose his real honour if it be risked for truth's
> sake, and placed in the Redeemer's hand.[56]

The Baptist Union turned against Charles and censured him in early 1888.[57] Some of Charles's own men joined the voices of his opponents. These men were graduates of his Pastors' College; men who had enjoyed the benefits of a solid theological education; men who regularly sat at his feet for instruction and fellowship; men Charles had poured his heart and life into. Their defection devastated him.

Charles started writing his devotional book *The Cheque Book of the Bank of Faith*, a book about God's promises, during the Down-Grade. Its preface is perhaps the most revealing of any of his other writings as to the personal heartbreak that he felt. He identified with the prophet Jeremiah's "sorrow which comes of disappointed love." Like Jeremiah, Charles "would have turned his people from their errors, but he would not himself quit the way of the Lord." Charles said, "For him [Jeremiah] there were words of deep sustaining power, which kept his mind from failing where nature unaided must have sunk." From a heart of "disappointed love" Charles wanted to comfort pastors: "I want to say to them in their trials—My brethren, God is good. He will not forsake you: he will bear you through."[58]

Susie wrote of the Down-Grade as the "deepest grief of his noble life."[59] In *C. H. Spurgeon's Autobiography,* Susie authored the chapter "The 'Down-Grade Controversy' from Mr. Spurgeon's Standpoint," to offer a tender yet truthful account[60] because she was concerned that Charles was being misrepresented. Susie was pained as she recounted the devastating controversy—so intense was the battle, so great were the losses.

And, it wasn't the Down-Grade alone that weighed on Charles during that time: his mother died in June, 1888; Susie suffered a severe setback with her health; and his own health sent him back to bed for a time. He wrote: "We have had a stormy voyage of late, both for our own barque and for our consort." Yet, he saw his suffering as God's provision for ultimate good. That said, his troubles mounted, and he felt the fire. "In the present instance it must be well, but the furnace has been fiercely hot."[61]

The Down-Grade Controversy is still debated today by Spurgeon scholars—though it is clear that Spurgeon was right concerning theological decline in the Baptist Union (by the beginning of the twentieth century, liberalism had claimed many former evangelicals), it is not as clear that he handled the controversy as well as he might have. Though he was still in his right mind—he was tired, death just years away, and he lacked the energy to be more personally present for the fight. Other questions linger: Did he draw his circle of friends too tightly leaving him surrounded by men who dared not question his methods? Should he have been more patient in his work for reformation?

Even among some who counted him as a great hero of the faith, there was concern that he was not at his best in controversy. Susie believed that he was faithful in his defense of the faith and, even in her weakened physical condition, her love for Charles sparked a fiery defensiveness. She could see no wrong in her husband. And Spurgeon's closest confidants urged him onward. Though well intentioned, his loyal supporters may have served him better by offering constructive criticism that could have equipped him in the long-term work of reform.[62] All said, Spurgeon was right to oppose theological liberalism.

One of the positive effects of the controversy is that it drew Charles and Susie even closer to one another, if such was possible. Even as he languished, he encouraged Susie via his letters: "We are safe in His hands. This is where I love to feel that I am, and that you are, and the dear boys, and the Church, and the College, and 'the Down-grade,' and all!"[63]

Yet, in the midst of the battle, Charles confessed to feeling weak, worthless, and bruised. He added, "There is no music in me now, there is a rift which lets out all the melody."[64] Let that sink in for a moment—Spurgeon was the most famous preacher in the world, many thousands came to faith in Christ through his ministry, orphans and widows had received the direct touch of his care, millions read his books and sermons, and Victorian London was transformed for good beneath his leadership; yet, the Prince of Preachers felt "worthless."

Susie fought the Down-Grade on three major fronts. First, she doubled down in her Book Fund ministry and reaffirmed her commitment to uphold the truth by sending doctrinally sound books to poor pastors. "Solid, old-fashioned, Scriptural, Puritanic theology alone goes forth from the Book Fund shelves," she wrote in 1887 at the beginning of the Controversy.[65] She wanted nothing to do with the "new thought" that was slowly eroding long-standing churches and theological institutions. Secondly, she fought the Down-Grade through her writing. Her reports in *The Sword and the Trowel* displayed her firm belief that pastors needed books that upheld the gospel preached by men such as John Bunyan and her husband. Thirdly, she fought the battle as she had all others that Charles was engaged in by wholeheartedly supporting her husband and not letting the pains of controversy get the best of her.

Though Charles lost the support of some of his old friends, his stature grew in the estimation of Susie, and her support was unwavering. She believed that his cause was right, and she grieved with Charles over the "doubt, and deliberate divergence from the plain paths of the old Gospel" demonstrated by so many.[66] Susie was an "immeasurable blessing" to Charles in this regard.[67]

Charles lamented those who had no such partner and friend as he had in Susie: "Where there is not this mutual affection, it deserves not the name of marriage . . . Without love, wedded life must be a real purgatory above ground."[68]

CHAPTER 5

Expressive Communication

JUST BEFORE THREE O'CLOCK on the afternoon of June 10, 1854, Charles Spurgeon, Susie Thompson, and a large circle of their friends from church were seated, amongst thousands of others, inside the new Crystal Palace building in Sydenham, South London. After great anticipation, the Palace was officially opened by a flourish of trumpets announcing the approach of Her Majesty, Queen Victoria. The queen, dressed in a light blue gown and wearing a white bonnet, walked slowly to the center of the dais. Prince Albert, to her left, wore the scarlet uniform of a field officer, and His Majesty, the King of Portugal, to her right, was dressed in regal attire. The royal children stood on the dais with their parents and various dignitaries.

The National Anthem rang forth, accompanied by the acclaimed soprano soloist Madam Clara Novello, whose voice filled every nook and cranny of the vast building. Pride expanded the chest of every Englishman in attendance as the anthem was zealously performed. When the music faded, a cannon strategically placed on the grounds outside thundered its approval. The queen was then seated upon her chair of state. Her charge was read, including her "earnest wish and hope that the bright anticipations which have been formed as to its future destiny may be completely realised, and that the wonderful structure and the treasures of art and knowledge, which it contains, may long continue to elevate and instruct, as well as to delight and to amuse, the minds of all classes of the people."[1]

After opening formalities and a tour, Victoria and her entourage returned to the dais as the orchestra delighted the crowd with the musical accompaniment to the words of Psalm 100. Joyful notes and melodious voices filled the building. The Archbishop of Canterbury then offered a blessing, after which the orchestra returned to its royal strains. Silence fell over the great facility, and the Marquis of Breadalbane stepped to the front announcing, "I am declared by her Majesty to declare this Palace opened." The crowd cheered and then was allowed to explore the exhibits throughout the vast structure.[2]

The Crystal Palace had first opened at Hyde Park in May of 1851 with a ceremony similar to the 1854 grand reopening attended by Charles and Susie in Sydenham, the new and permanent location. The colossal building of glass and steel housed exhibits from around the world and symbolized the power, wealth, and creativity of the nation. The Great Exhibition, housed in the Crystal Palace, was something like the World's Fair and included displays and demonstrations of cutting-edge inventions, creations, art, and technology from around the globe. Though the nation had entered the Crimean War by declaring war on Russia in March, and Charles Dickens had begun publishing *Hard Times* as a serial, the Crystal Palace presented a message to the world that its greatest city, London, was facing its challenges confidently.

As the grand processional inside of the Crystal Palace passed by that June day, Charles and Susie, seated side by side, watched the inaugural events unfold. It is likely that Charles had secured the seating arrangement at Susie's side in order that his clever plan of revealing his feelings for her might come to fruition. The air was electric, but one imagines that Charles's scheme captured more of his attention than the royal family occupying center-stage for the ceremonies.

Charles had been the pastor of the New Park Street Chapel for less than three months. He was young and ambitious and, by his own admission, sometimes prideful. Susie Thompson was a regular attendee of the church. She remembered that they sat inside of the Crystal Palace talking, laughing, and amusing themselves as they waited for the procession to pass by.[3] But the excitement of the grand processional was about to fade into the background.

Charles leaned toward Susie and handed her a book of poetry: Martin Tupper's *Proverbial Philosophy*. He pointed out one poem in particular, and then whispered in her ear, "What do you think of the poet's suggestion in those verses?"

Quietly, Susie read the lines:

> Seek a good wife of thy God, for she is the best gift of
>   His providence;
> Yet ask not in bold confidence that which He hath not
>   promised;
> Thou knowest not His good will; be thy prayer then
>   submission thereunto,
> And leave thy petition to His mercy, assured that He will
>   deal well with thee.

If thou are to have a wife of thy youth, she is now living
   on the earth;
Therefore think of her, and pray for her weal.[4]

Susie quickly realized that Charles was interested in more than her opinion of a poem.

Charles and Susie's friendship had grown exponentially since at least mid-April of that year, when he had learned that she was concerned about her spiritual condition. Though their communication had often been lighthearted, much of their earliest conversation was related to the more important matter of Susie's conversion and spirituality. Soon after Charles's early encounters with Susie, he became smitten with her beauty, her cultural expertise, and especially her interest in spiritual things. Charles's feelings for Susie were deepening, yet he wasn't ready to share them. "I loved you once but feared that you might not be an heir of Heaven," Charles later admitted in a letter to Susie. Once he was assured that she was indeed a Christian, he felt freedom to reveal to Susie his affections for her.[5]

As Susie contemplated the words of the poem, the love that had been growing inside of Charles now beat in her own heart. Just six months prior, on December 18, 1853, Susie had first seen Charles and heard him preach. She certainly couldn't have anticipated then the excitement that now flushed her cheeks.

One wonders if Charles had any doubt as to how Susie would react to his subtle suggestion conveyed via Tupper's poem. Always thoughtful, perhaps Charles discerned that just maybe Susie was now as positively inclined to him as he was to her. Regardless, he risked both his heart and their friendship by his bold intimation. Charles then took his most daring step. In a soft, low voice, he whispered in her ear, "Do you pray for him who is to be your husband?"[6]

Later, Susie couldn't recall if she actually answered Charles's question, but she remembered that her heart raced, her cheeks were flushed, and her eyes were bright. Though surprised at how things had unfolded, she was happy.[7] Two Victorians in love—not much different in their excitement than any loving couple today.

Any doubts that Charles may have previously entertained about how Susie would respond were put to rest as they walked around the palace and even down by the lake—and that for an extended time. He could tell by her demeanor that she was pleased.

Charles and Susie's care for each other rapidly deepened, and soon afterwards, Susie knew she was in love with Charles and he with her. In the days following, Susie and Charles walked together around their favorite London sites and enjoyed a weekly rendez-vous at the Crystal Palace. What were Charles and Susie's dates like? One night each week he came to her home and edited his previous sermon for publication (such sounds a bit boring to modern ears, but Susie found it helpful and enjoyable) and another day each week was their meeting at the fountain inside of the Crystal Palace. Their main joy was in simply being together.

A couple months later, in August of 1854, Charles wrote to his friend James S. Watts that the Crystal Palace was a favorite haunt he'd like to share: "I shall rejoice to take your arm one day, and survey its beauties with you."[8] No doubt, the Palace was in large part a favorite place of Charles's because it was there that he first declared his love to Susie.

The Palace was a sentimental place for Susie. She wondered as she reflected on that June night, "Was there ever quite such bliss on earth before?"[9] This from a young woman who had strolled the streets of Paris in her teenage years and who had enjoyed many of life's finer treasures. Susie found something more precious to her than the romantic atmosphere of Paris's and London's high society; Susie found love, and the world's greatest cities and experiences could not hold a candle to Charles.

That August, Charles proposed to Susie in her grandfather's garden, a place that Susie referred to from that point on as "a paradise of happiness."[10] There, on that simple and nondescript square of ground, Charles and Susie pledged their hearts to one another, and one of Christian history's greatest love stories flourished.

COMMUNICATION:
A KEY TO MARITAL HAPPINESS

Charles and Susie's romance both before and after their marriage was punctuated with simple verbal and handwritten communication or, in the case of the grand reopening of the Crystal Palace, via a book. At the beginning of his friendship with Susie, though Charles could not have helped noticing her beauty, his foremost concern was to help her spiritually. His first recorded writing to her was his inscription on his gift to her of *The Pilgrim's Progress*: "Miss Thompson with desires for her progress in the blessed pilgrimage. From C H Spurgeon, April 20, 1854."[11] Charles's gift led to deeper conversations about Susie's spiritual state, and, at some point afterwards, he recognized in Susie a potential life partner and fellow pilgrim.

Effective communication, so vital in relationships, is often cited as one of the greatest challenges confronting married couples. Charles was a master communicator as his creativity of expression at the opening of the Crystal Palace demonstrated. During Charles and Susie's lifetime, the way that couples kept in touch with one another when they were separated was through either regular mail (postcard or letter) or telegram. The telephone was not in use until 1876, and, even then, it was only gradually employed due to limited availability. Imagine a world without that, let alone the Internet, social media, email, and texting we take for granted today. With Charles's travels causing him to be gone from home each week, he and Susie were dependent on writing letters. In his early London years, Charles preached an average twelve times a week. Though he often preached within proximity of his home, he was also regularly away from London. Therefore, written correspondence was their main means of keeping in contact during their engagement and marriage.

After 1840, postage was cheap, and the mail traveled swiftly throughout England. Though there are only few extant letters that he and Susie exchanged, each one provides some important insight into their relationship. We will return to their letter writing in the last section of this chapter.

SHALL I READ TO YOU?

"Shall I read to you to-night, dear?"[12] Susie's question to Charles usually came on Sunday evenings when he was exhausted from spending much of the day at church, preaching and ministering to the multitude that attended the services each week. Weary and often discouraged at the end of the Lord's Day, Charles needed comfort.

Susie asked, "Will you have a page or two of good George Herbert?" Charles responded, "Yes, that will be very refreshing, wifey; I shall like that." He then chose a portion for Susie to "read slowly and with many pauses," so he could interpret the "sweet mysteries hidden within the gracious words." Susie presumed that her husband enjoyed the book all the more as he expounded to her the "precious truths enwrapped in Herbert's quaint verse;—anyhow, the time [was] delightfully spent."[13]

Such readings were not brief, but, as Susie described, "I read on and on for an hour or more, till the peace of heaven flows into our souls, and the tired servant of the King of kings loses his sense of fatigue, and rejoices after his toil."[14]

Sometimes Charles's spirits were low because he felt cold spiritually. Susie said that he was occasionally not only tired but also depressed. He felt, on some Sundays, that he had failed in his preaching and that he had not urged sinners to repent fervently enough. In Susie's presence he asked God to forgive him. On such occasions, Charles asked Susie to read a soul-piercing book to him. He imagined such reading would "quicken" his "sluggish heart." As Susie read, she was often interrupted by Charles's "heart-sobs." His grief over his perceived sin in light of the goodness of God was unbearable. Susie, unable to contain herself, wept with him out of love for him and a desire to share his grief.[15]

Susie's encouragement of Charles wrought benefits for it rejuvenated Charles in his efforts toward cultivating a joyful and godly home.[16] Though good order was important to Charles, his greater desire was that his home be plentifully supplied with love and happiness. He knew that it was grace, not rules, that sweetened family life. Therefore, his pleasure was in pleasing Susie. Charles had witnessed enough mean and unthoughtful husbands to see how destructive unkindness was to family joy.[17] He was happy with his Susie. He wrote to a friend just over a month after his wedding this simple heading: "*Wife*, first-rate; beloved by all my people, we have good reason mutually to rejoice."[18]

Positive communication extended to Charles and Susie's twin sons Charles Jr. and Thomas. They instilled biblical wisdom to them by teaching them hymns when they were young and writing to them when they were older and away from home. Charles considered family "the grandest of all institutions."[19] He taught his students at the Pastors' College that the leader of a family "usually finds that his pre-eminence is one of superior self-denial, rather than self-assertion."[20] Charles's verbal and nonverbal communication with Susie and their children was most clear in his humility and sensitivity to the needs of his household.

PEN, PAPER, AND LETTERS HOME

Though the Victorian era was characterized by technological changes that included more rapid communication, Charles's preference was to use a dip pen and to express his thoughts and feelings on paper. Unless gout laid siege on his body, his penmanship was lovely. His letters to Susie overflowed with humor, personal anecdotes, encouragements, requests for prayer, and his intimate feelings about her. Charles could have chosen fountain pens for his writing instrument, as they were available during his lifetime, but using a dip pen likely helped him to write slowly and thoughtfully: pause, dip, write. And, he didn't like fountain pens as he considered them "indistinct" and "more like a pencil than a pen."[21]

In a lecture on prayer at the Pastors' College, Charles connected prayer to writing: "If you can dip your pens into your hearts, appealing in earnestness to the Lord, you will write well; and if you can gather on your knees at the gate of heaven, you will not fail to speak well."[22] Though Charles was referencing the writing of sermons, the application is also apropos for letter writing.

His letters to Susie were centered on God. In 1869, as she was recovering from surgery, Charles addressed Susie as "My own dear

Sufferer." He encouraged, "Oh, may the ever-merciful God be pleased to give you ease!"[23] He closed that letter with these words:

> I must not write more; and, indeed, matter runs short, except the old, old story of a love, which grieves over you, and would fain work a miracle, and raise you up to perfect health. I fear the heat afflicts you. Well did the elder say to John in Patmos, concerning those who are before the throne of God, "neither shall the sun light on them, nor any heat." Yours to love in life, and death, and eternally, C.H.S.[24]

Susie's letters to Charles lifted his spirits. Though her letters are not available today, he acknowledged their importance while he was alive: "My Precious Love, your dearly-prized note came safely to hand, and verily it did excel all I have ever read, even from your own loving pen."[25]

Though letter writing was the preeminent means of communication during the Victorian age, it has mostly fallen out of vogue in our day. "In the future old love letters may not be found in boxes in the attic, but rather circulating through the Internet, if people care to look for them," wrote Webster Newbold, professor of English at Ball State University. In 2010, he noted that the typical home received a personal letter about every seven weeks. Two decades prior to that, it was once every two weeks.[26] A 2018 *New York Times* article states that the average American household receives just ten pieces of personal mail a year. The author cites a survey that indicates that half of British children have never sent a handwritten letter.[27] The situation was opposite in Spurgeon's day.

Correspondence by post was much different after 1840 as the mailman often came to a residence several times in one day. Perhaps modern couples can learn from Charles and Susie's example. Whereas email, texting, and other forms of digital communication are helpful tools to keep in touch with one's spouse, arguably they are poor substitutes for the love and thoughtfulness that pen and paper can communicate.

Communication, whether spoken or written, was offered generously, for both Charles and Susie *enjoyed* discussing ministry, nature, travel, art, books, and plans. Charles wrote, "Every word I write is a pleasure to me as much as it ever can be to you."[28]

Charles and Susie's epistles were like a renewal of their covenant with one another. A couple of excerpts illustrate Charles's covenant perspective: "Every year casts out another anchor to hold me even more firmly to you," and "All my heart remains in your keeping."[29] Susie remembered, "Every day his dear messages came to me, except, of course, when a long railway journey intervened."[30] Every day! Today we send a text or call home, but Charles took the time to write a thoughtful letter to Susie—every day.

Charles knew that his letters encouraged Susie—they were therapeutic. His personal correspondence was not stylistically brilliant but, as Susie confessed, his letters were "simply a loving husband's daily notes to his sick wife, a record of his journeyings gladly and faithfully preserved in with the sole object of pleasing her, and relieving her of sorrowful loneliness."[31]

Charles's notes reflect his deep love and romantic affections for his "wifey." Susie's debilitating physical illness wore her down. Charles spoke courage into her life through his letters: "You, my darling, have been enabled to do this; and though the weary, wary pain bows you down, you will be able to possess your soul in patience even unto the end."[32] Charles pointed Susie to the comfort of God and reminded her that her work was important. "Some of those well-ripened apples which housewives bring forth amid the chill, leafless days of winter, God hath in reserve for thee; wherefore, be of good courage, my sweetheart!"[33] Each note was ripe with encouragement, comfort, cheer, and sweet expressions.

On one of Charles's trips, he recollected the time that Susie had been with him, visiting the same places:

> We saw all, and then went to the Luxembourg Station to continue our journey, by Waterloo, to Namur. O "days of auld lang syne," how ye flashed before me, especially when we rode along by the Meuse and Juy to Liege, and thence to Chadfontaine, Verviers, and Aix-la-Chapelle! Alas! My dearest bides at home; and I, like a lone knight, can but remember the ladye of my love, for she rides not at my side as aforetime![34]

Many miles separated Charles from Susie, but his letters united them. Of course, he never imagined that his tender, sweet, and blushingly romantic letters to Susie would one day be read by others. What would Charles think if he knew that we were reading these words? "My heart flies to my wifey; I have just kissed my hand to her. God bless her! Loads of love I telegraph by the soul-wire."[35] He wouldn't mind at all; he would have wanted others to know how much he loved and admired Susie. Charles toured the greatest cathedrals and viewed natural treasures of the Continent; however, his experiences, after Susie's sickness and concurrent inability to travel, were always lacking something—or rather, *someone*. His joy, therefore, was never quite complete when he was separated from Susie. Letters helped to close the gap that geography placed between them.

He worried about Susie and longed to hear good reports from her; he was gloomy when he did not know how she was doing. When her letters came and he learned that she was fine, he thanked God.[36] Yet he missed Susie, and his loneliness was exacerbated when, for example, he was in Venice, a place he and Susie had enjoyed together some years earlier. As Charles wrote about riding in a gondola along the Grand Canal, his thoughts rushed back to the exact track he and Susie had traveled together in past days. Each pleasure he enjoyed was mingled with longing for Susie.

His letters often signaled his emptiness without Susie: "Could you but have been there, it would have been as much of Paradise as this earth can ever yield."[37] Every place Charles visited, such as a palace ruin in Rome, which he compared to London's Crystal Palace, reminded him of Susie and their home and experiences together.[38] It was from Rome that he wrote, "I love my love amidst all these great thoughts. She is my palace, my throne, my empress, my Rome, my world; yet I have more, my Saviour, my Heaven! Bless you, my own!"[39]

Charles's word pictures stirred Susie's imagination. On one occasion she shared one of his letters with their sons. Fascinated by his picturesque writing, she told them: "There, dear boys, is not that a fine description? That simple language Papa uses, and yet how forcible. One can almost see the scenes he pictures."[40] With a letter from Charles in hand, Susie felt almost as if she could see what he was seeing and that she was there at his side. Almost.

Charles counted Susie's letters to him as "precious." He writes of a day in which he received two notes from her. He told Susie that they were more valuable to him "than all the gems of ancient or modern art." Susie's letters were as "pure as alabaster, far more precious than porphryr or verd antique; no mention shall be made of malachite or onyx, for love surpasses them all, to Charles."[41] From Pompeii, Charles affectionately declared, "I must cease writing to-night, but I continue to breathe loving assurances to my sweet wifey."[42]

A couple of final examples display the joy of Charles and Susie's relationship: "I send tons of love to you, hot as fresh lava,"[43] and, "Now, my wifey, this brings galleons of love to you, and a cargo of kisses lies under the hatches ... God give thee still thy daily patience while He sees fit to send thee pain; but, oh! may He remove the affliction and send healing to thee, and brighter days to us both! Nevertheless, His will be done!"[44] Charles considered it "dear work" when he was "communing with [his] darling by the pen."[45]

CHAPTER 6

Learning Together

ON WEDNESDAYS, CHARLES OFTEN ATTEMPTED to steal away from the city for a time of relaxation. On those days, it was not unusual for him to rise even earlier than normal to get some work done. On one such occasion, he met his friend William Williams at the train station for a day trip to the country. He asked Williams if he had done any work that morning. Williams said that he rose and was at work from 6:30 a.m. until 9 a.m. Charles, in fun, one-upped his friend, "Oh, I was in my study at half past four. I had five hours of solid work before I left, so I think I may enjoy my holiday."[1]

Though he was able to make this trip with his friend, his carefully laid plans were sometimes hindered. Word would get out, even miles from London, that he was nearby, and requests would pour in for him to preach or to meet with someone. He had a difficult time—it was almost impossible for him to say "no" to such appeals, and only rarely did he refuse. When friends encouraged him to politely turn down invitations, Spurgeon retorted that the matter was not as simple as that. "It pains me to refuse anyone; and to decline to preach is so contrary to all my heart's promptings, that I had rather be flogged than feel compelled to do it."[2]

It was challenging for Susie to catch a moment alone with Charles—he had such little margin in his calendar. What it meant to be the wife of Charles Haddon Spurgeon, in part, was solitariness for long periods of time. And when Charles was in proximity to Susie, he was often so singularly focused on his work that he could pay her but little attention at times. J. H. Harrald, Spurgeon's primary assistant, mused, "Surely there never was a busier life than his; not an atom more of sacred service could have been crowded into it."[3]

Though Spurgeon attempted to keep Wednesdays open for rest, work often crept in, and his personal time slithered away. Replying to letters was one task that occupied him on his days off. He was mostly happy to issue a response, but in some cases, the solicitations that he received containing questions could have been figured out by the letter's author on their own. Such letters led him to complain a bit; yet his generous heart usually squelched his complaints, and he answered such correspondences. To one such query, he encouraged the writer to see his pastor for counsel.[4] Spurgeon lamented to his son Charles, "I am only a poor clerk, driving the pen hour after hour; here is another whole morning gone, and nothing done but letters! letters! letters!"[5] Historian Iain Murray noted that one of Spurgeon's elders alone preserved about eighty letters from Charles.[6] Letter writing, up to five hundred per week, was but one of many of Charles's responsibilities.

The result of Charles not diligently taking time off and/or skipping other times for rest was that his health broke down more rapidly, and he was sidelined from his normal responsibilities. One might easily imagine that Susie was disappointed with Charles's flurry of activity when he had scheduled a respite, expecting Charles to rest or to visit with his friends, or to spend extended time with her. However, he often felt that he had to keep on working. Susie didn't complain when he was busy at home—at least when he was at home, he was in proximity to her. That, in itself, provided opportunity for her to engage Charles in conversation.

Charles sat in his wooden leather chair in his study across from his friend and biographer G. Holden Pike and confessed that though he was blessed with a beautiful home and property, he rarely had opportunity to enjoy his garden—a place he loved and that was a refuge for him. His garden helped to unshackle him from some of his burdens. He said God didn't begrudge him the enjoyment of his garden—the garden was a gift from God. Charles was wistful but thankful as he considered his little paradise, "It is about the only luxury in which I indulge. I am very hard worked. . . . I have neither time nor strength to move about and find refreshment in variety and change as others do; but I have my garden with its flowers and its fine prospects, and I praise Him for it."[7] "But I have my garden." Beautiful words, hauntingly poignant words, spoken almost dreamily; words revealing that Charles's extraordinary life squeezed out many pleasures—but, he said, "I have my garden."

Pike was concerned about his friend: "The pressure seemed to become more and more overwhelming; and it became more and more evident that the cause of the ailments which now became more frequent and more painful was mental rather than physical."[8] Charles's trials were *both* mental and physical and the one exacerbated the other. His continuous work caused him to break down all the more.

Sometimes the effects from his physical breakdowns confined him to bed. Though Susie was at his side when he was home and delighted to care for him, his ability to interact with her was diminished. Occasionally his doctors sent him packing to warmer weather, which usually brought relief to his tired mind and hurting body, even as the separation deepened Susie's sense of isolation from him. Charles enjoyed his southern ventures while also suffering homesickness. One of his friends said that Charles was "a man who loved his home and was happy in it." And of Susie, he said, "Then, as all the world knows, the pastor was happy in having a wife whose tastes and aspirations were in sympathy with his own."[9] The effects of Charles's tiring schedule on his health and his time certainly touched his marriage in painful ways.

Charles accomplished mountainous tasks in part because of the "efficient helpers in various departments of his service."[10] Yet, even with all of his assistants, he outworked them all. He was a precise organizer and could easily put the willing hands of his assistants to work, but it was said that he was so "quick in his work that he could probably do single-handed so much as all of them combined could accomplish."[11]

Susie was the assistant he appreciated most, and when she worked by his side several good things happened: (1) they had time together, (2) she was a true assistant and her help was invaluable, and (3) they learned together.

It shouldn't be imagined that Charles's work was drudgery to him; he loved to serve Christ. And, it's not accurate to assume that he and Susie did not spend extended times together along with their weekly interactions; they seized every opportunity that they could, and in these moments—scarce as they sometimes were—they learned together.

On Saturdays, guests frequented the Spurgeons' home. Prior to their arriving, Susie, when able, accompanied Charles for a walk around the property to their small summerhouse (more like a closed-in gazebo that Charles named "Out of This World").[12] Charles entertained their visitors with humorous stories. He led tours of the barn, gardens, and even introduced his friends to his horses. Charles had the unique ability of telling a story and then, without missing a beat, kneeling to pray for and with his guests.

After enjoyable hours that included happy conversations around tea, the guests, along with the domestic servants, all gathered in Charles's study for family worship. And during those times, perhaps even more than when he was preaching from the pulpit or instructing students at his college, he was personable and relaxed. Susie listened, watched, and learned from him.

> It was at these seasons that my beloved's prayers were remarkable for their tender childlikeness, their spiritual pathos, and their intense devotion. He seemed to come as near to God as a little child to a loving father, and we were often moved to tears as he talked thus face to face with his Lord. At six-o'clock every visitor left, for Mr. Spurgeon would often playfully say, "Now dear friends, I must bid you 'Good-bye,' and turn you out of this study; you know what a number of chickens I have to scratch for, and I want to give them a good meal to-morrow [those who would hear him preach]." So, with a hearty "God bless you!" he shook hands with them, and shut himself to companionship with his God.[13]

When the clock struck six, Charles retired to his study, and his guests were on their way. Susie listened for Charles's call, "Will you come and help me to-night, wifey?" She said, "The service was one which an angel might have coveted." Susie read to Charles from a stack of books and commentaries that he had laid out and opened to particular sections relevant to the sermon he was crafting. She was not only able to minister *to* Charles during those times, but *her* theological study was enhanced as she learned from writers of antiquity points of theology that otherwise might have been lost to her.[14]

Reading commentaries to Charles was a happy work and instructive work for Susie. She explained:

> There comes delightful pauses in my reading, when
> the book is laid down, and I listen to the dear voice of
> my beloved as he explains what I cannot understand,
> or unfolds meanings which I fail to see . . . How shall
> I sufficiently thank God for this drink of the brook by
> the way, this "holy place" within my home where the
> Lord deigns to meet with me, and draw out my heart in
> adoration and worship?[15]

All of Charles's preparation for Sunday's sermons was not done on Saturday evenings as is commonly believed. During the week, he carried a notebook with him everywhere and recorded any insight from nature, people, trains, animals, or reading—anything at all that he might use in a sermon or drop into a book he was writing. However, it was on Saturday evenings that he made his final selection of a text, studied the passage in the original languages, read from commentaries, and put together an outline.

Sometimes Charles struggled to choose a text for his sermon. When that happened, he walked out of his study troubled and asked for Susie's input. "Wifey, what shall I do? God has not given me my text yet." Susie comforted him as much as she was able. "It was, to me, a cause for peculiar thankfulness when I was able to suggest to him a passage from which he could preach; and afterwards, in referring to the sermon, he seemed pleased to say, 'You gave me that text.'"[16] How many sermons did Susie have a hand in sending down the line? The answer is unknown, but her suggested texts often found their way into the pulpit. Charles viewed Susie's ideas as the hand of God directing him to a particular passage.

Along with receiving the benefits of assisting Charles with sermon preparation, Susie's participation of reading commentaries out loud also aided him in more personal ways. His soul was soothed by the words that fell from the lips of the woman he loved as she read from a book he loved that pointed him to the Savior he loved.

Labors on the Lord's Day for any faithful pastor are emotionally draining and physically exhausting. Charles was no different. His emotions were tender and fragile and that—along with a litany of other concerns—often set him back on a Sunday night after church services were over. Charles asked his students at the Pastors' College, "How often, on Lord's Day evenings, do we feel as if life were completely washed out of us! After pouring out our souls over our congregations, we feel like empty earthen pitchers which a child might break."[17] Susie's remedy for her beleaguered husband was to refill his heart with glorious truths about God. She declared that such thoughts "are sure to induce great longings after Him, great faith in Him, and great love towards Him; and thus, being filled with His fullness we soar above and beyond all the earthly distractions and disturbances which surround us, and seek to cast us down."[18]

Whether it was Puritan theology or poetry, Charles was refreshed by Susie's gentle voice. Sometimes one minute turned into sixty or more minutes of Susie reading, time that was "delightfully spent."[19] The time passed quickly, for both Charles and Susie learned, and were refreshed, and their marriage was strengthened for they were together.

A pastor's wife is expected to attend worship services and, like other members of the church, to serve Christ on the Lord's Day. Though Susie was in her place at church each Lord's Day from her engagement to Charles in 1854 through most of 1867, after that, due to her debilitating health struggles, she seldom attended church again. Such was painful to her for she longed to be with the people of God in corporate worship. Therefore, since she was confined to home while the church gathered, the time she had to read, both the Bible and other books, and to participate in Charles's sermon preparation was vital to her own growth in godliness. There was no other avenue for Susie after 1868 to "hear" sermons, except when she and Charles labored together in the Word of God. Susie would have been thrilled to have the technology of our day, so that she could watch live-streamed services from the Metropolitan Tabernacle and listen to the heavenly voice of Charles expounding the Scripture.

On one occasion, Susie was privy to Charles's preaching via an extraordinary experience. It was a Saturday evening in April of 1856, just three months after their marriage, and Charles was attempting to pull his sermon together for Sunday morning. His wrestlings to interpret the passage were intense, and even after poring over numerous commentaries, he was frustrated and unable to discern the passage's meaning.

Charles ran his hands through his hair and rubbed his face—but it was no use, he simply could not get to the meaning of Psalm 110:3. Susie urged him to go to bed and wake up early. She promised to make sure that he was up in plenty of time to work on his sermon before church. Charles took Susie's advice and then slept like a child. At some point in the night, Susie heard him talking in his sleep. She sat up straight, listened carefully, and realized that he was talking about the text that he had been wrestling with. Not only that—he was preaching the text, clearly and with attention to its meaning. Susie dared not leave the bed to fetch a pen—she was afraid that she might miss something from Charles's exposition. So, she listened.

And she prayed that God would help her to remember what her husband was saying—if she could memorize his words, then she could recite them to him in the morning. She kept repeating his statements until she fell asleep. Charles woke up startled—upset that Susie had not awakened him—and anxious over what he would do. Susie gently calmed him and told him what had happened.

> "Listen, beloved,"... and I told him all I had heard. "Why! that's just what I wanted," he exclaimed; "that is the true explanation of the whole verse! And you say I preached it in my sleep?" "It is wonderful," he repeated again and again, and we both praised the Lord for so remarkable a manifestation of His power and love. Joyfully my dear one went down to his study, and prepared this God-given sermon.[20]

When he finally delivered the sermon on Sunday morning, April 13, he declared to his congregation the difficulty he had faced preparing the message:

> Never verse in the Scripture has puzzled me more than this to find out its meaning and its connection. In reading it over hastily, at first sight, it may appear very easy; but if you search into it very carefully you will find you can with difficulty string the words together, or give them any intelligible meaning. I have taken down all the commentators I have in my possession; I find they all give a meaning to the words, but not a soul of them— not even Dr. Gill—gives a connected meaning to the whole sentence.[21]

This sermon, "A Willing People and an Immutable Leader," can still be read today—a sermon God gave to Charles in his sleep, a sermon he and Susie believed God had provided his fatigued servant.

CREATION AS THEIR CLASSROOM

It was not at all infrequent, especially during their days of robust health, for Charles and Susie to wander together throughout their gardens, and down the street near their home. Tenderly, Charles took Susie's hand into his own as they strolled the grounds of their lovely home. During their walks, they usually discovered in nature something fresh that they could make ready use of for a spiritual application—a lesson in a plant or a bird high above in a tree. Both wrote in their books of lessons learned from observation. Charles found spiritual illustrations in animals, trees, thunderstorms, and various objects along their pathway. Susie wrote of truths discovered while watching a plant grow or from meditating on a drop of water collected in the center of a flower.

Charles told students at his college, "If you keep your eyes open, you will not see even a dog following his master, nor a mouse peeping up from his hole, nor will you hear even a gentle scratching behind the wainscot, without getting something to weave into your sermons if your faculties are all on the alert."[22] His friend William Williams witnessed the great preacher's personal practice of this as he enjoyed intimate access to the Spurgeon home:

> Mr. Spurgeon delighted in his garden at Westwood. He
> knew every plant and flower in his conservatories; he
> used to linger over them as over verses of the Bible when
> he was commenting, "Is not that exquisite? Look at the
> veins and colors in these leaves; don't you think God
> has put His own thoughts in them? The plant has His
> laughable thoughts . . . this His loving thoughts . . . this
> His serious ones. All nature is full of God. His autograph
> is on every leaf and in every flower."[23]

Charles and Susie's idea of true religion allowed them to see, savor, and enjoy the beauties of God that saturated all of creation. Charles lamented a Christian man's perspective who, while sailing down a famous river, "closed his eyes lest the picturesque beauties of the scene should divert his mind from Scriptural topics." He regarded that man's *spiritual* mindset as very unspiritual and said that it "savours of absurdity."[24]

Susie shared Charles's outlook. One evening she took a stroll along the grounds of Westwood to gather roses "to preserve their perfumed leaves." She described how her roses had stood up to the "fervid glances of the sun, and the hot kisses of the South wind" and yet, in the midst of their trial, she found them "blooming in clusters of unusual beauty . . . apparently as fresh, and cool, and invigorated as if the blessed rain for which we had prayed had already fallen." As she gathered roses, she noticed one bloom was "besprinkled with water." She then recognized that the "shake of the rose" had brought forth water from its "inmost recesses." The reservoir of water, contained within *all* of her roses, had strengthened them "against the heat of the day" and "refreshed them with water from within."[25] She applied her discovery to Christians struggling under the "heat and burden of the day":

> Think a moment on my roses and how tenderly God has provided for their need. Could He be less thoughtful for thine? Has He made such wonderful provision for their sustenance and refreshment during the days of drought, and "forgotten to be gracious" to thee? Ah, no! Thou well knowest it is not so.[26]

Like her husband, Susie saw scriptural parallels in nature. In the account, she reflects on Psalm 77:9: "Hath God forgotten to be gracious? Hath he in anger shut up his tender mercies? Selah."

LEARNING THROUGH PROMOTING EDUCATION

Another way that Charles and Susie were enlightened as a couple was through facilitating the learning of others. The Pastors' College, which Charles had started (1855), Susie supported (1856), and they both sustained for a lengthy period from their own funds, was Charles's crown jewel in the midst of his other ministries. For many years, Charles and Susie entertained students at their homes, first on New Kent Road, then at Nightingale Lane, and finally at Westwood. They worked together for the annual college conference as well. Susie carefully chose books that she inscribed and gave to each college conference attendee. Her familiarity with the best in Christian literature only deepened her understanding of God and connected her with the sorts of books that influenced Charles.

So erudite were Charles and Susie together that a book Charles authored was mistakenly attributed to Susie. A young pastor wrote to Susie soliciting *Lectures to My Students*; he wanted "the lectures written by you." Susie said that he underlined the words "lest there should be any mistake about such precious productions!" She recalled, "My husband made the richest fun of this blundering request. 'Oh,' he said, 'they're not published yet! That is a pity! They are first-rate, but they are only orally delivered.'"[27] Charles and Susie were interdependent; yet, they were a team in work and in learning. She said, "Ah! but there is, thank God, only love and peace in 'home sweet home!'"

The Spurgeon home was sweet in a thousand ways, and, whether during their afternoon jaunts or more formal study times together, learning was a pleasure when Charles and Susie learned together.

CHAPTER 7

A Time to Laugh

ON THE FINAL SUNDAY OF DECEMBER 1888, Charles was in
Mentone, France, at a church service. After preaching, he and
some friends rested at a home that overlooked the Mediterranean
Sea. Making his way down a carpeted marble staircase, Charles's
walking stick slipped, and he tumbled down the steps. Two teeth
were knocked out and some coins from his pocket fell out and
landed in his boots. His first remark after being helped up was,
"Painless dentistry!"

Though he made fun in the midst of his misfortune, he was
injured and laid up in bed for a few days. It was just like Charles to
turn his accident into an occasion for humor, while his concerned
friends fretted about his health. He also used his unwitting descent
down the stairs to poke fun at his Down-Grade opponents. He
told his friends to "let the down-graders know how terrible is a fall

from the high places of the Lord's truth." As for Charles, he hoped to keep his "footing to the end."[1]

Charles's humor both reflected happiness *in* his marriage and brought happiness *to* his union with Susie. Why is a jocular spirit so important in marriage? The Bible teaches, "A merry heart doeth good like a medicine: but a broken spirit drieth the bones" (Proverbs 17:22). Every marriage has a few rocks along the passageway; the Spurgeons' marriage was no different. However, without godly humor, a marriage will be dry—inflexible and cold. Though Charles was widely acclaimed as one of the world's great preachers, his humility and zest for life freed him to laugh—and, to laugh at himself. His friends testified to his humor and his wife delighted in it.

Charles's close friend William Williams wrote of him,

> What a bubbling fountain of humour Mr. Spurgeon had! I had laughed more, I verily believe, when in his company than during all the rest of my life besides. He had the most fascinating gift of laughter I ever knew in any man, and he had also the greatest ability for making all who heard him laugh with him.[2]

The Pastors' College students waited anxiously each week for their president's Friday afternoon lecture. Spurgeon instructed his students on everything from the preacher's voice, to the effects of depression, to humor. No subject relevant to ministry, family, or personal piety was off limits. In a lecture he opined, "I like an honest laugh; true humour can be sanctified, and those who can stir men to smile can also move them to weep."[3] Charles preferred that his hearers smile rather than sleep through his sermons. His humor was not crass or irreverent; his was holy humor. He believed a merry heart was pleasing to God. Ecclesiastes 3:4 teaches that there is "a time to laugh." Charles and Susie embraced that verse in their marriage and certainly their humor helped them to face hardship with hopefulness.

Charles maintained, "Cheerfulness is the sunshine of the heart."[4] And his cheerfulness shone through in his responses to the many questions asked of him in conversation. When asked if he thought a man who learned to play a trumpet could be a Christian, Charles replied, "He may be; but I question whether the man living next door can!"[5] On another occasion, Charles was looking over a life insurance application and one of the questions regarded whether the applicant had been "afflicted with any Fits or Convulsions." Charles responded, "No, unless convulsions of laughter are meant."[6]

How could Spurgeon laugh so frequently when he had so many concerns? He faced mountainous challenges with his health, dealt with theological controversy, cared greatly for Susie's affliction, and lived with a burden that sinners were lost and needed Christ. But he laughed *and* he cried—sometimes there is a fine line between the two. He believed that one ought to have gospel-sanctified emotions, and, therefore, the gospel was central to his view of laughter. "There are times when, if I sit alone and think of the grace of God to me, the most undeserving of all His creatures, I am ready to laugh and cry at the same time for joy that ever the Lord should have looked in love and favor upon me."[7]

Helmut Thielicke contended, "Spurgeon's cheerfulness is not evidence of his having the natural charisma of 'a good sense of humor' . . . his humor rather bears witness to the grace that is at work in him."[8] Thielicke's statement is telling as to how Spurgeon viewed humor as an outworking of sanctification.

When Susie was unable to submit a Book Fund report for

publication, she wanted her "dear Mr. Editor" to tell his readers that though her hands were too shaky to write that her mouth was "filled with laughter," and her "tongue with singing." She laughed because she reflected on God's love and God's sovereignty—no shaking hands would cause her to doubt God's purposes or His care for her. She believed God graciously sustained her to do the work He wanted her to do.[9] Though her sickness occasionally side-lined her, she found that God's grace allowed her to continue, and even laugh, nonetheless. Susie saw laughter as an indicator of faith: to laugh in the face of hard times was a great testimony of her faith in God.

Laughter was a means of praising God for providing for all of her needs through generous donors who supported the Book Fund ministry. Laughter was not incongruent with the gospel; it was a natural outgrowth of knowing and loving God. Susie, like Charles, viewed godly laughter as holy work.

PURE FUN

A chapter entitled "Pure Fun" was included in *C. H. Spurgeon's Autobiography*. There Susie revealed that during the Annual Conference for students and alumni of the Pastors' College, Charles invited men to join him at home on Friday afternoon and evening for fellowship. One of his requests at those gatherings was for the men to repeat, for Susie's pleasure, the witty anecdotes that he had uttered during conference week.[10] Very simply, he wanted Susie to laugh; and she didn't disappoint. Because Susie's admiration was important to him, Charles felt validated when Susie laughed at his witticisms.

So deep was the storehouse of his humor that he could draw

from it on almost any occasion and even turn a mistake into an opportunity to poke fun, especially at himself. For example, he mispronounced a man's name when greeting him. "How are you, Mr. Partridge?" The gentleman responded, "Patridge." Charles recovered with humor, "Ah, well, I promise you that I will make game of you no more."[11]

Charles bemoaned dour Christians whose philosophy intimated that wit and humor are sinful and should be avoided by pious people.[12] He assumed a counter perspective, considering humor a necessary duty. He shrugged off "melancholy critics who think everything solemn should be sad, and that anything approaching a pleasantry must be wicked."[13] Some Christians refused to laugh and have fun on a Sunday, equating the Sabbath Day with soberness. Charles considered laughter both wholesome and holy regardless of the day of the week.[14] "I do believe in my heart that there may be as much holiness in a laugh as in a cry; and that, sometimes to laugh is the better thing of the two," he told his students.[15]

The proposition that laughter might be a holy engagement was a concept not much considered by the higher-brow church attenders in London's upper-crust churches. Spurgeon's congregation, however, loved their pastor and laughed with him. One of his friends said that "his wit was as abundant as his wisdom, and he often conveyed his wisdom by means of his wit.[16] Another friend remembered that "between playfulness and the prayer there seemed to be no abrupt transition, no discord, no incongruity,—but all was perfect harmony and happiness."[17]

For Charles and Susie, all of life and all of God's varied gifts were sacred, including laughter. Their marriage was a breath of fresh air in the midst of a Victorian religious culture that was sometimes stiff, formal, and even stifling. Charles and Susie made no sharp division between the secular and the sacred. There was sacred and sinful, but *all* of life was to be lived for the glory of God. And so, they laughed.

Like Martin Luther, one of his historical heroes, Spurgeon believed that all lawful activities could be joyfully employed and enjoyed by Christians. Luther's humor, though arguably not always proper, was a reflection of his happy heart. And one of his favorite activities was to gather with his wife and children and sing happily around the piano. Spurgeon concurred.

One of their friends said that Charles "showed how it was possible for the highest spirituality to find a fitting exemplification in the brightest and cheeriest character."[18] Other friends indicated that "there was not the slightest incongruity after one of his brilliant witticisms, which had set the whole company laughing, in hearing him say, 'Let us pray,' for both the merriment and the devotion were sanctified."[19]

For example, Charles took issue with the hymn writer who tweaked a hymn based on Psalm 100 by inserting "fear" in place of "mirth" in the third line of the verse. Charles's preferred rendering was:

> All people that on earth do dwell,
> Sing to the Lord with cheerful voice;
> Him serve with *mirth*, His praise forth tell;
> Come ye before Him and rejoice.[20]

Mirth is a feeling of amusement often expressed through laughter. Spurgeon's theology fit with that idea, and though he used humor sparingly in the pulpit, he did use it—and did so unapologetically. The practice, however, earned him some criticism. To one critic, Charles responded, "If you had known how many others [witticisms] I kept back, you would not have found fault with that one; and only the last great day will reveal how many were first attracted by some playful reference or amusing anecdote which was like the bait to the fish, and concealed the hook on which they were happily caught."[21]

Charles thought that the proper use of humor was not a hindrance but a help in evangelism and teaching. Such a mindset was shocking to many churchgoers and religious critics in Victorian England, though the culture was not without appreciation of humor and satire. The wildly popular periodical *Punch*, a humor/satire publication, is evidence that even Victorians laughed. Though Charles was often the butt of jokes in that missive, he mostly took it in stride as one who could dish it out as well; he even named one of his pug dogs Punch. Spurgeon laughed at *Punch*, and he knew how to land a good-natured one himself.

Funny Letters

Sometime after 1868, Charles wrote in a cheering letter to his homebound wife of "head-gear" women were wearing on the streets of Botzen. He included funny sketches of ladies' hats and bonnets that caught his attention while he was out walking. "Now, sweetheart," he added, "may these trifles amuse you; *I count it a holy work to draw them*, if they cause you but one happy smile."[22]

Susie compared Charles's happy letters to those of the "Psalters and Missals of the Middle Ages, when the hand of some pious man toiled day after day to decorate the vellum pages,—simply to prove the love of his heart and witness to the truth of his devotion." Susie imagined that Charles's humorous and loving words and sketches carried the same implied meaning for her.[23]

Charles always considered it his "delight" to please Susie.[24]

Making her laugh was a way he tried to achieve that. In a letter to her, he wrote of touring the Glyptothek in Munich: "We have been to the Glyptothek, a fine museum of statuary; but, really, after one has seen a few thousand nude figures, one feels content without any more anatomical models in stone."[25]

Musical Humor

Although Spurgeon thought musical accompaniment was inappropriate for congregational worship in his church, and though he didn't make a big issue of it with other pastors, he would have preferred that no church employ instruments during their worship services. However, his view was not shared by many of his friends.

He preached in churches across the Continent, some with and some without organs. Once he pointed to the organ at a church and announced to the congregation, "I look upon that as an innovation; and if I were here, I should want it to be an outovation, and then we would have an ovation over its departure."[26] Winsomely, and wittily, he made his point.

Delighting Others

Charles frequently instigated uproarious laughter wherever he was. And his skillful usage of humor was disarming, even to those in high places of leadership.

In the fall of 1868, Charles attended the Autumnal Meetings of the Baptist Union at Bristol where he and a couple other prominent men were at breakfast with a large group of students.

Charles was the life of the gathering because of his "hilarious spirit." It was said that "his good nature and jollity infected everybody and broke up the reserve and timidity common to most of us when in the presence of distinguished persons." Rev. George E.

Rees observed,

> The house was full of mirth and laughter from the hour
> he entered it . . . . Mr. Spurgeon began to talk in an
> informal manner about things in general. One foot was
> on a chair and one hand in his pocket, and his face wore
> that contagious brightness so common to it in his earlier
> years. Very soon the lecture room became a scene of
> convulsive laughter and tears.[27]

Charles took a trip with his friend William Williams who was asked by a Mr. Duncan if he knew how to shoot. Williams replied, "I was almost born with a gun in my hand"; so, it was determined that Williams would show off his skill the next day. Later in the evening, Charles turned to Williams and said, "Oh, Mr. Williams, I have asked and obtained permission from Mr. Duncan for you to shoot that fine stag in the meadow; see, he is lying there now." Charles egged Williams on, telling him that Duncan had promised him the venison to take home with him. Williams crept up to within forty yards of the animal only to discover that the stag was bronze. Williams turned around to find that Charles, co-conspirator of the prank, was "laughing with all of his might."[28]

Joy in Marriage

For Charles and Susie, laughter was just one more way that they could praise God in their marriage. Charles had a high view of women and of marriage. He didn't appreciate the inappropriate jokes that some men told about women. He wrote, "If I were not married today, and saw a suitable partner, I would be married tomorrow morning before breakfast."[29]

Charles loved being married: "John Ploughman is a sociable

soul, and could not do in a house by himself." Chastising unloving husbands, he said, "He who ill-treats his wife ought to be whipped at the cart tail, and would not I like a cut at him!"[30] Charles and Susie believed that "marriages are made in heaven" and the person is a fool who poisons his home with a bad attitude or mistreatment of their spouse.[31] Charles saw no reason for the honeymoon to ever come to an end—"When hearts agree, there joy will be" because marriage should be "merry-age."[32]

Susie described Charles as her "head," but said that he ruled with a gentle demeanor. Charles addressed a bride at her marriage ceremony by stating, "The husband is the head of the wife. Don't you try to be the head; but you be the neck, then you can turn the head whichever way you like."[33] Though Charles was a strong leader at home, he was ever sensitive to the desires of the "neck" and did all he could to facilitate her wishes and needs, including the need to make her laugh.

Godly laughter was an evidence of Charles and Susie's sanctification and of joy in their marriage. Yet, it wasn't just married couples who were to display such delight—but all Christians. Joyless Christianity was an oxymoron to the Spurgeons.

In a sermon he delivered on January 1, 1882, titled "Shining Christians," Charles said, "I am most of all vexed with myself whenever my own joy burns dimly, for we who have the light of the glory of God ought to have shining faces." His reasoning was gathered from the gospel. "We have been forgiven; we are God's children; we are on the way to heaven; then surely, if anybody's mouth ought to be full of laughter, and if any tongue should be turned to sweetest music, it should certainly be ours."[34]

CHAPTER 8

Habits of a Creative Couple

ON A TRIP TO MENTONE, Charles struck up a conversation with a medical doctor. The eminent physician didn't recognize the famous preacher. As the two talked, the subject turned to disease and remedies. The doctor was astonished at the breadth and depth of knowledge about physiology and medical treatment that Spurgeon commanded. The doctor later said, "He is the most remarkable man I have ever met . . . He seems to me to know as much about the human body and almost every form of disease as any medical man I know. He would have been a splendid physician."[1]

Charles seemed to have an encyclopedic knowledge of almost everything from architecture to geography. William Williams asserted that those who had conversed with Spurgeon "were impressed with the wide range of his interests and his knowledge. He spoke of trees as if he had studied nothing else; he seemed as familiar with the stars as a schoolmaster is with the alphabet and he discussed physiology and anatomy with the knowledge of a trained physician."[2]

Unique powers of observation along with voracious reading habits nourished Charles's creative mind. He read six substantive volumes a week, including biographies of great preachers and leaders. He imbibed all of the vast tomes of the English Puritans,[3] and he studied Thomas Manton, Martin Luther, John Calvin, and John Wesley. He devoured the works of "the Tinker from Bedford," John Bunyan, and he encouraged his students to have *The Pilgrim's Progress* "at your finger ends."[4] Though his lack of formal training in an advanced educational institution had caused some to be rather dismissive of him, his ability to read fast and to comprehend much afforded him a vast treasury of knowledge.[5]

Charles's twelve thousand-volume library was stocked with theology books as well as works on birds, humor, smoking, poetry, history, literature, and medicine, including a volume on gynecology, collected due to Susie's particular affliction.[6] He had all of Ruskin's volumes and a full set of Dickens. He knew where each of his books was located in his library and, if needing to reference a particular passage from one of them, he knew the page number from memory. He had a tremendous mental capacity, able to hold eight different thoughts in his mind at the same time while preaching. He described his brain as a library with shelves filled with thoughts that he could retrieve at will and interact with all at the same time. He enjoyed and engaged life at a very high level.

From his vast array of experiences, his reading, his friendships, and his astute observation skills, it is no surprise that Charles was a creative man, all of which contributed to his loving demeanor toward Susie. He was creative as a preacher and a writer using language brimming with descriptiveness. His stellar memory allowed him to bring his life experiences and observations into his sermons and books as fit illustrations and anecdotes.

Writing books and preaching sermons aside, Charles was at his best when creatively expressing his love for Susie. This was one ingredient that made his marriage happy.

When postcards were first marketed, Charles used them to write love notes to Susie. He liked using the open card because his unblushing expressions of affection were exposed to any in the mail service who might be curious enough to read them. On the first postcard he mailed to Susie, he wrote up-and-down-and-up instead of the usual left-to-right. The paragraph below is the text followed by part of the letter as Charles wrote it.

October 1, 1870   Nightingale Lane, Clapham

My dear wife, as this is the first day of the new cards, I
write to you upon the first one I use. The more eyes there
may be engaged in curiously reading my note, the better,
for I should like all the world to know that you are the
best wife to be met within the whole of her Majesty's
dominions. Long may you be spared to be a blessing
to your happy husband, a guide to your children, and a
worthy example to all wives. With health restored may
[be] relative to the whole of comfort there. Your presence
is the light, beauty, and soul of the whole. With love,
your loving husband.

My	engaged . . .
dear	may be
wife,	there
as	eyes

this	more
is	The
the	I use.
first	one
day	first
of	the very
the	upon
new	you
cards,	to
I	write[7]

Spurgeon's repository of knowledge, blended with his gifted-ness, served him well in his marriage. Susie, too, was well-read, well-traveled—and an able conversationalist. One of the reasons that she was the perfect wife for Charles was that she entered marriage with thrilling experiences gained from London and Paris—experiences that fascinated Charles. The Spurgeons' lively discussions included art, theology, cathedrals, travel, and a plethora of other subjects. Dinner conversations were not boring at the Spurgeons' home.

Due to their unique circumstances, they *had* to be creative in order to make the most of their sparse time together. A moment here and there together, and then Charles was off again on a min-istry trip. Usually Charles's travel experiences were positive, though there were notable exceptions. In 1861, Charles was preaching 120 miles away in the city of Bristol. Two thousand people were packed inside the building and hundreds stood outside, clamoring to enter, but there was no room—the doors had to be bolted to prevent utter chaos. The crowd outside grew rowdy and threatening; they threw rocks at the building. Charles was unnerved.

The trauma of the Music Hall Disaster of 1856 had a way of rearing its ugly head at inopportune times; such was the case on this evening. During prior services when the crowd was large and a feeling of trouble settled upon Charles, he had to nerve himself before preaching.

Under duress, Charles reached the pulpit. He surveyed the congregation and said, "I am excessively nervous—I might say unwell—for the fear of a great crowd. If any noise or alarm should arise, let no one be alarmed, but remain self-possessed, and there can be no fear of danger."[8]

The aggressive throng outside remained loud and boisterous. Spurgeon, still agitated, paused the proceedings for a few minutes. After restarting the service, the crowd banged on the building again. Charles placed his head in his hands and leaned against the rail of the pulpit. He was shaken. He asked that the meeting be postponed until the next time he was in Bristol. The audience inside, however, urged him to carry on. Incapable of refusing, he submitted to their request and preached as best he could. Finally, the service ended, and Spurgeon was able to leave Bristol the next morning and return to London.[9]

Such situations—along with every other burden he bore, caused both Susie and his friends great concern. Charles, however, was committed to serving Jesus, no matter the cost to his health. For all of his ministry, he was reluctant to curtail his schedule for his theology drove him to active engagement. He said: "I believe that a Christian man is generally right when he is doing more than he can."[10] The cost of such constant exertion was significant.

A. Cunningham Burley wrote that Charles and Susie's sons had very limited engagement with their father during their childhood. "His [Spurgeon's] time was mortgaged, weeks and months ahead, and long spaces were allowed to go by with little more than a passing glance and a few hurried words from [their] father."[11] Such, at least for a time, created a "restraint" when the sons didn't talk much with their father. However, there was no lack of love between father and sons. Son Charles intimated that his regard for and closeness to Charles deepened as the years went on. "Father and son came at last to enjoy each other's society and success."[12] There was a constant tension that Charles felt between time spent in his public ministry, which he treasured, and his family that he loved. Such is not uncommon for any husband or father. Not driven by blind ambition, Charles simply wanted to serve Christ fully, unquestionably, and wholeheartedly.

Later in his life, when embroiled in the Down-Grade Controversy, he wrote,

> I may care about myself till I grow morbid; I may watch over my own feelings till I feel nothing; and I may lament my own weakness till I grow almost too weak to lament. It will be far more profitable for me to become unselfish, and out of love to my Lord Jesus begin to care for the souls of those around me. My tank is getting very low; no fresh rain comes to fill it; what shall I do? I will pull the plug, and let its contents run out to water the withering plants around me. What do I see? My cistern seems to fill as it flows. A secret spring is at work. While all was stagnant the fresh spring was sealed; but as my stock flows out to water others the Lord thinketh upon me.[13]

Charles believed that by emptying himself in service, God would replenish him. He cited Proverbs 11:25: "He that watereth shall be watered also himself."[14] Though he sometimes collapsed emotionally due to his responsibilities, his normal habit was to press onward in his duties. Charles said, "I could scarcely content myself even for five minutes without trying to do something for Christ."[15] His home life with Susie emboldened him as he faced those duties—she was a life-restoring stream of fresh water to him.

But she sacrificed much—not because of Charles's demands, but because of her love. Charles and Susie creatively and joyfully supported one another during such times, fed by the "secret spring at work" in their marriage and in their happy and industrious home.

Much has been made of Charles's busy schedule but not as much of Susie's. She had imagined a time when she would cease her work with the Book Fund, but she became convicted that she must continue. Susie didn't see any way she could go from zealous activity to resting from her labors. She had letters to answer, and she feared "the weight of a reproachful conscience" if she retired from her work.[16] How could she stop? God gave her strength "to continue working every day, all the day long."[17] She said, "I must open wide the storehouse, feed hungry minds, and fill up the poor pastors' book-shelves while the plenty lasts."[18]

Charles and Susie's vigorous activities derive directly from their theological underpinnings. They believed that God created them to serve others, and they wanted to be faithful. While we applaud them for their service, we might also imagine that with both of them so active, Charles and Susie must have had a mysterious secret to their marital bliss. We have considered several ingredients of their happiness: biblical spirituality, mutual support, laughter, etc., served to strengthen and spice up their relationship. There is no "secret" in those things, but all those elements of their happy marriage required creativity—a creativity that could even be seen in the spirit of their home.

WESTWOOD: BEAUTY AND GRACE

Charles and Susie's last home, Westwood, is their most-remembered home today.

William Williams wrote that one word described the Spurgeons' home-life at Westwood, —*beautiful*. After living at their Nightingale Lane address for twenty-three years, Charles and Susie moved to Westwood in 1880 and remained there until their deaths. Williams visited Westwood frequently, and he witnessed, first-hand, the sweet relationship between Charles and Susie.

> Mr. Spurgeon loved his wife with a tenderness and intensity of affection I have seldom known equaled. Mrs. Spurgeon was a great sufferer during all the years I visited the home. One of the many lessons I learned at Westwood was that grace can indeed teach us "to suffer and be strong"; to be strong in affection to the Father.[19]

Biographer George Stevenson remarked on Spurgeon's marriage, "It may serve as a model worthy of the imitation of many Christians, and particularly of Christian ministers."[20] How did Charles and Susie cultivate such a happy marriage? They were deliberate in their approach. Spurgeon declared:

> Marriage is not a relationship of original consanguinity. It is contracted between two persons who may, during the early part of their lives, have been entire strangers to one another; they may scarcely have looked each other in the face, excepting during the few months that preceded their nuptials. The families may have had no previous acquaintances; they may have lived afar off as the very antipodes. One may have been opulent, and in possession of vast domains, and the other may have been indigent, and reduced to straitened circumstances. Genealogies do not regulate it: disparities do not hinder it. The connection is not of natural birth but of voluntary contract or covenant.[21]

Charles and Susie entered into such a covenant. Though strangers to one another before their first meeting and having few things in common, their differing backgrounds actually worked in their favor. All differences of background and circumstances could have been problematic had Charles and Susie not been diligent in communication, united in priorities, thoughtful of one another, and creative in seizing time to spend together.

Their relationship was enhanced by their positive attitudes. The record is absent of a fierce argument, silent treatment, or any other unhealthy emotional or physical action. They worked together, and each delighted in the joy of the other. Charles wrote that he "never was half so happy before I was a married man, as I am now." He said about Susie: "If there is only one good wife in the whole-world, I've got her."[22] On a separate occasion, Charles received pushback from an anonymous critic concerning a critique Charles had made about eccentric preachers. The critic told him to "look at home," meaning to look in the mirror. Charles turned the critic's statement into an opportunity to praise his actual home life with Susie. "I do look at home, and I am glad that I have such a happy home to look at."[23]

When first seeing their new home at Westwood, located on Beulah Hill in South London, Susie was reminded of Bunyan's description of Immanuel's Land near the Celestial City in *The Pilgrim's Progress*.[24] In those days, before London was as far-reaching, with towering buildings and sprawling residences, as it is today, Charles and Susie sometimes could see St. Paul's Cathedral from Westwood, seven miles away. On especially clear days, they viewed the towers of Windsor.[25] Westwood had its own tower that allowed Charles and Susie a magnificent view of the horizon, a sight that they enjoyed contemplating.

Susie's inventive decorating touch turned their large house into a warm and comfortable refuge. William Williams remarked that "the taste displayed in all the arrangements would have satisfied the most aesthetic, while the gardens, grounds, and conservatories were ever a charm to the eye, and, when [Charles] was there to point out this beautiful feature and the other, a delight to the mind."[26]

One of the congenial features of Westwood was its nearness to the Crystal Palace. What sweet and romantic reminders of Charles's earliest expression of love for Susie the Palace held. If Charles was the "People's Preacher," as he was sometimes called, The Crystal Palace was the "People's Palace" because it was accessible to rich and poor. In 1857, Charles had addressed nearly twenty-five thousand people, the largest crowd of his ministry, in the Palace. Charles and Susie must have considered it a kind providence that their last home was less than two miles from the place where their early romance budded. Perhaps on a sunny winter's day when the trees were bare, they could see one of the towers of the Palace rising above the trees from their own tower.

Not only was Westwood in proximity to the Crystal Palace, it was also near a church that Susie was involved in from 1888 until her death—Beulah Baptist Church, Thornton Heath. And it was less than two miles away from West Norwood Cemetery where Charles was buried in February of 1892 and Susie in October 1903.

In 1885, *The Pall Mall Gazette* published an article on the Spurgeons' house and family. The reporter provided a picturesque narrative of the flowerbeds that adorned the property. He described Charles's library with its floor-to-ceiling bookshelves, packed to capacity with books and decorated with various relics that Spurgeon had collected over the years. From the décor inside the house to the lovely little pond outside occupied by swans, Westwood reflected the Spurgeons' personalities. The horse stable was so clean that

Charles said, "You might eat your dinner off the floor."[27] Over the stalls were signs bearing the names of their two horses, Brownie and Beauty. Along with the fernery on the property were ten milk cows serving a milk industry that Susie administered; she donated the proceeds of the milk sales to a local ministry.[28]

The *Pall Mall* reporter was surprised when Susie encouraged him to stay for tea. He wrote, "I was willingly persuaded; we had pears, peaches, plums, and honey, all from his [Spurgeon's] own garden . . . after tea, the family, with the servants, were called together for family prayers." Before he left, Susie gave the reporter a tour of the house, as well as the workroom where she wrote all the correspondence for the Book Fund, and also where the books were stored and the parcels were prepared to send to pastors. Charles, joining the tour, pointed to numerous pictures of scenes from the Protestant Reformation hanging in the hallway. The reporter noted Charles had four or five hundred. "He delights in all that illustrates and honors these heroes—Calvin, Beza, Luther, and the rest of the Lord's chosen men at arms."[29]

Celebrating Marriage at Home

Westwood was always bustling with activity. Books and letters were constantly being mailed, visitors were entertained, the staff had to be given direction, and Charles was studying or writing much of the time. Westwood operated in a disciplined manner. However, changes to their schedule were not uncommon—especially when Charles or Susie or both were sick. Such times required, if they were to maintain any sense of normalcy in their marriage, a creative and flexible approach. For example, Charles was unwilling for special occasions to go uncelebrated, even when his routine had to be reoriented.

On their silver wedding anniversary (January 8), there was to be a congratulatory meeting at the Metropolitan Tabernacle on Monday, January 10, 1881. However, the celebration at the church had to be cancelled because Charles was sick. Though plans were disappointed, Charles imaginatively devised a new plan to celebrate Susie and their anniversary at Westwood on February 2 (and to connect it with the scheduled deacon's meeting). The invitation was handwritten by Charles and, as best Susie could remember, it was the only time that he signed a letter with their "united initials." The invitation read:

> Westwood
> Beulah Hill
> Upper Norwood
> Jan. 31, 1881
>
> Dear Friend,
>
> Lest you should forget it, I beg to remind you that the Deacons Meeting will commence here at 5 on Wednesday next.
>
> At 6:30, we will meet for tea, & after tea, we hope to celebrate with you our silver wedding with great thankfulness to God.
>
> Please come as early as you can that we may get through business before tea.
>
> Yours heartily,
>
> C. H. & S. Spurgeon.[30]

William Olney and a Mr. Carr served as spokesmen on behalf of their fellow deacons. They gave a glowing testimony of Charles and Susie and their sons. Afterwards, the group continued with a time of fellowship and joined the Spurgeons for family worship, led by Charles with his "usual fervor and impressiveness."[31]

From the beginning of their marriage, Charles and Susie's sweet relationship was a testimony to others of God's grace. Their ability to turn hindered plans into opportunities helped them to keep their marriage fresh.

One of their friends sent a letter that was kept by Charles and treasured by Susie that points to their happiness. The letter, Susie said, "sweetly links the beginning of our wedded life with the twenty-fifth anniversary of our marriage."

> My Dear Friend,
>
> My mind reverts to the month of January, twenty-five years ago, when a certain newly married juvenile Pastor and his wife came to me for a few days, and solaced themselves in their mutual love for each other at my house.
>
> Many things have happened since that time; but their faithfulness and their affection for each other have not been impaired; and now that they are about to celebrate their silver wedding, I ask permission to remind them of those early days, and to add my hearty congratulations at this auspicious period.
>
> May the 8th of January, 1881, ring in a strain of joyful music, over the strings of the past, assuring them that "golden days" are yet to come, even before they "walk the golden streets." So prays,—
>
> Their old friend and well-wisher,
>
> J. S. Watts.[32]

After Charles's death Susie reflected on her marriage to Charles—with smiles and tears: "Ah, sweetheart! Was there ever one like thee?"[33] Those days of young love, Susie intimated, never ended and were not diminished.

GOD MOVES IN CREATIVE WAYS

Though Charles spared no effort to express his love for Susie, his intentions sometimes exceeded his abilities. But God moved in extraordinary ways to do what Charles would have done, had he been able.

When Susie was sick in bed and preparing for surgery in 1868–1869, Charles asked her many times, "What can I bring you, wifey?" Susie rarely responded because she was content with all that she had, except for good health—something Charles couldn't provide.

However, eventually she offered a very specific, but playful, request in response to Charles's enquiry: "I should like an opal ring, and a piping bullfinch!"

Charles could think of no way to fulfill her desires, but he and Susie had a good laugh at her request.

One Sunday after church, Charles, face beaming, walked into Susie's room with a look of delight. He held out a tiny box, then opened it, removed a beautiful opal ring, and happily placed it on Susie's finger.

Smiling, Charles said, "There is your opal ring, my darling." The ring had come to Charles via an elderly lady he had visited in her sickness. This lady had sent a note to the Tabernacle indicating her desire to give Mrs. Spurgeon "a small present, and could somebody be sent to her to receive it?" Charles and Susie rejoiced at God's sweet provision in granting an "unnecessary gratification to His dear sick one."[34]

A short time later Susie was transported to Brighton for her surgery, an event that she referred to as a crisis. One evening, Charles made the trip down from London to visit her, and he was carrying with him a large package. Inside was a cage containing a lovely piping bullfinch! Susie was overwhelmed with emotions. A lady whose husband was sick could no longer care for the bird and asked Charles to give it to Mrs. Spurgeon. She had no idea that Susie wanted such a gift. When Charles told her of Susie's desire, she rejoiced with him and wept over God's kindness.

Looking deep into Susie's eyes Charles said, "I think you are one of your Heavenly Father's spoiled children, and He just gives you whatever you ask for."[35]

....

Charles and Susie shared with one another the generous spirit that God displayed toward each of them. Whether it was Susie making sure Charles had the best accommodations in their house for his study, or Charles mailing Susie a letter in a biscuit can (which he did on at least one occasion), they were joyfully creative and generous toward one another.

When Susie returned home from her surgery, Charles had fitted a room for her near his study. He spared no expense to make sure she was comfortable during her convalescence. The *Autobiography* provides this account.

> Never will the rapture with which he welcomed her
> home be forgotten, nor the joyful pride with which he
> pointed out all the arrangements he had made so that
> her captivity should have every possible compensation
> and alleviation. There was a cunningly-contrived
> cupboard in one corner of the room, into which he had

gathered all the details of his loving care for her. When the doors were opened, a dainty washing apparatus was disclosed, with hot and cold water laid on, so that no fatigue in ascending and descending the stairways should be necessary, and even the towels were embroidered with her name. He had thought of *everything*; and there were such tender touches of devoted love upon all the surroundings of the little room that no words can describe her emotions when first she gazed upon them and afterwards when she proved by practical experience, their exceeding usefulness and value.[36]

Although his duties still required him to travel during this season, Charles wrote to Susie, sending her "wagon-loads of sweet love, and ton weights of affection," and he prayed for her healing as he was "counting the days" until he could see her again.[37] Creative, beautiful, and hopeful was Charles and Susie's marriage.

CHAPTER 9

A LETTER ARRIVED AT THE SPURGEONS' HOME in February of 1879 from their friend Thomas Johnson, an African-American missionary in Africa.[1] Johnson had been a slave in Virginia for twenty-eight years before his release near the end of the Civil War. "Tell dear Mrs. Spurgeon to keep inching along, Jesus Christ 'll come by-and-by," Johnson wrote.

The letter took Susie back to an evening when Johnson, along with his wife, Henrietta, and his friend C. H. Richardson and his wife, visited the Spurgeons to say goodbye before leaving for Africa's mission field. After encouraging the departing group, Charles asked them to sing for Susie "some of the strange, sweet songs of their captivity."

Susie recalled, "My heart was especially attracted by a peculiar air, to which they sang as a refrain these most curious words:—

'Keep inching along, keep inching along
Like a poor inch worm,—
Jesus Christ 'll come by-and-by.'"[2]

Susie enquired about the history of the song, and Thompson told his story of bondage in Virginia when he and other slaves huddled together holding hands and whispering the song out of fear that if their masters heard them singing, a beating would follow. They then sang the song again "*in whispers*," as they had during their slavery.[3] Susie never forgot "that pitiful hushing of their voices. There was not a dry eye in the little company when the song was ended; but we wiped our tears away, soon remembering that the cause for sorrow no longer existed."[4]

Thomas Johnson was born into slavery in 1836. His book, *Twenty-Eight Years a Slave or The Story of My Life in Three Continents* recounts his experiences as a slave, a pastor, and a student at Spurgeon's Pastors' College, as well as his life as a missionary in Africa and an evangelist. As a slave he was "illiterate," and he was "owned as a mere chattel and treated as such," but after he came to a saving knowledge of Christ on June 6, 1857, he was received into "Christian society . . . as a brother and a man."[5]

Johnson longed to take the gospel to his homeland. Though he had but scant ability to count, read, or write, he relied on what his mother had earlier taught him: the alphabet, counting to a hundred, and the Lord's Prayer.[6] Believing Queen Victoria of England was a friend of freedom, she became a heroine in Johnson's eyes. Though attempting several escapes, with the hope to get to Canada and beneath Victoria's reign, he was never successful, and his failures intensified his grief.

In 1863, Johnson had married Henrietta Thompson. Though often separated at the whims of their owners, the couple loved one another deeply. Johnson was emancipated in 1865, just prior to the conclusion of the Civil War. Describing his three "birthdays," he wrote:

Born August 7th, 1836—a "Thing."
Born again (John iii. 7) June 1857—a Child of God.
Born into human liberty, April 3rd, 1865—a Free Man.[7]

After his conversion, Johnson said, "No longer was I a mere chattel, but a man, free in body, free in soul; praise the Lord."[8]

. . . .

After Johnson's release, he traveled to New York where he was given funds to send for his wife; and then to Chicago. In both places, the Lord put influential people in his pathway, people who helped him along the way. He longed for a formal course of learning to undergird his desire to preach the gospel in Africa. While pastoring in Denver City, he leaned heavily on the writings of Spurgeon.

Johnson had first encountered Spurgeon's ministry while a slave, having overheard his masters discussing the famous London pastor. They didn't speak very highly of Spurgeon because of his antislavery views. In the southern states, some mocked Charles, burned his books, and threatened to hang him if he were to ever venture into the southland. Though Charles's stand against slavery put his life in danger, he never wavered from his views, even refusing to knowingly take communion with a slave-owner. Though Spurgeon admired and learned from theologians and preachers, such as Jonathan Edwards and George Whitfield, who came before him and who were slave owners, he denounced the evils of slavery.

Eventually, Johnson returned to Chicago and was encouraged

to visit England and take a course of study for ministry preparation, something Johnson had long yearned to do. Thomas and Henrietta sailed for England and arrived in Liverpool on September 1, 1876. From Manchester, Johnson's friend Hind Smith wrote to Spurgeon requesting admittance for Johnson into the Pastors' College to audit the lectures. Spurgeon responded with characteristic compassion: "Dear Mr. Hind Smith,—Yes, let the dear man come." This opened the door for Johnson's eventual acceptance as a full student at the college, and it led to his becoming dear friends of both Charles and Susie Spurgeon.[9]

The Johnsons moved to London in December of 1876, and Thomas began his course at the college. After his first meeting with Spurgeon, he recalled,

> His first words set me at ease, but his sympathetic
> kindness was beyond my highest hope. He took me by
> the hand, asked me a few questions, and wished me
> success. The fear all vanished, and I felt I had been talking
> to a dear loving friend. I at once fell in love with dear Mr.
> Spurgeon, I know not how to express my feelings about
> this first meeting, and can only say that I felt so happy in
> his presence, and so at home with him, that I could not
> help saying, "Well, thank God he is my friend."[10]

Eventually plans were made for Thomas and Henrietta to sail to Africa, and the Spurgeons' warm and inviting home made the perfect place for a sendoff before their journey. Though the missionaries' time in Africa brought many joys, their team experienced sorrows too, including the death of Henrietta.

Susie wrote of Mrs. Johnson's death:

News comes from Africa of the death of Mrs. Johnson, one of the dear souls who sang so sweetly to us before leaving for missionary work there, and who joined in sending the message to me, "keep inching along." She is now singing the new song and has full realization of the blessedness of being "forever with the Lord." Stricken with the fatal fever, she has laid down her life in the land of her fathers, without having had much time to tell "the sweet story of old" to those for whose sake she bravely dared danger and death. We weep not for her; Jesus has come and taken her to Himself, and her bliss is perfect; but the desolate heart of her husband claims our sympathy and fervent prayers. Encompassed by danger, exposed to scorching heat by day, and deadly damps by night, weakened by fever and sorely cast down by the loss of his dearest earthly companion, our poor brother surely needs that we should "speak for him to the King" now in the time of his need and overwhelming distress. One feels that a return message to him could scarcely bear a fitter termination than the words which came over sea to us: "Keep inching along, Jesus will come by and by."[11]

Due to his diminishing health, Johnson returned to England in January of 1880; eventually he went back to America, a letter of commendation from Spurgeon in hand and a stack of books from Susie. Charles also gave him £10 and said, "If you don't get on, let us know. We will not forget you."[12]

One thing remained constant: Johnson's friendship with Charles and Susie and their love and compassion for him. In February 1892, Johnson was back in England and attended Charles's funeral. Though grieved over the loss of his friend, he simply said, "God never makes a mistake."[13] A few years later in 1903, he was also at Susie's funeral. He wrote, "On October 22nd, 1903, dear Mrs.

Spurgeon passed to her rest, and by her departure I lost one of my most kind and helpful friends."[14]

Charles and Susie never forgot their friend who urged them in his letter to "keep inching along," and, evidenced by Johnson's presence at both of their funerals, he never forgot Charles and Susie or their compassion toward him.

COMPASSION FOR ALL

Johnson's story illustrates the tender hearts of Charles and Susie and how they together shared in alleviating the pain, sorrow, poverty, and lack of opportunity that afflicted many people who crossed their paths. The stories of their work with their orphanages, the Pastors Aid Fund, Mrs. Spurgeon's Book Fund, and many others of their benevolent works all are saturated with the kindness of Charles and Susie. And, their work is a part of their love story—a narrative of Charles and Susie together helping the needy. Early in Charles's London ministry, it was the orphans who captured his heart.

Throughout London, many orphans sought cover in alleys and beneath rudimentary shelters. Charles likely witnessed something of their plight during his first evening in the city on December 17, 1853. Susie had also often seen poor and helpless children struggling for survival. These encounters eventually led to the Spurgeons' founding of two orphanages—one for boys (1869) and one for girls (1879)—built around a cottage family model rather than a more traditional dormitory plan. During Susie's years of health, she often visited the orphanages with Charles, especially at Christmastime, to the delight of the children. To their great excitement, Charles always had a pocketful of coins and candy for the boys and girls. They often cheered for him as he approached.

In total, sixty-six benevolent ministries were connected to the Metropolitan Tabernacle, including almshouses for the elderly. The almshouses were a part of the church (then pastored by John Rippon) when Charles arrived in 1854. When the houses were relocated to a site near the Metropolitan Tabernacle, Charles and Susie displayed staggering generosity. For years, out of their personal budget, they paid all of the heating, lighting, and other costs of the seventeen residences.[15]

Charles and Susie led by example, opening their home, their wallet, and their hands in service to others. London would have been a much darker city had Charles Spurgeon never accepted the call to the church there—and if he had never married Susie. Charles and Susie together were a powerful force of compassion for a city besought with many moral challenges.

Author Mike Nicholls writes that during the Victorian era Christians were invested in philanthropic enterprises "inspired by a faith in the worth of the soul of every man, woman, and child. Each person mattered, but many still lived and worked in conditions hard to imagine today, badly paid, badly housed, and badly fed."[16] Charles and Susie set out to make a difference as an outgrowth of their commitment to the gospel. For Susie, her priority was Mrs. Spurgeon's Book Fund and its corresponding ministries. Charles's two main benevolent interests were the Pastors' College and the orphanages. Yet Charles and Susie were together involved in all of the overall ministries of their church.

COMPASSION STARTS AT HOME

The Spurgeons' solicitude toward needy people was the fruit of their love for a compassionate God . . . and of their love for one another.

They often testified to the goodness of God to them; how could they fail to extend such kindness to others? One biographer described Charles and Susie's marriage by their "knowledge of what was deepest and best in each other." He wrote, "The result was that they came ever nearer one to the other in the sacred depths of their being. Nor were they truly happy except in each other's society."[17] Their happiness in one another was foundational to their concern for others.

Compassion started at the Spurgeons' home. When Charles wept, Susie attempted to dry his tears. When Susie was confined to bed, Charles saw to it that her every need, and many of her wants, were met. And when their sicknesses required them to be separated from one another, they prayed and sent cheering and consolatory cards and letters. Charles never allowed Susie to drift from his mind. The both of them together and their ministry to others reflect deep truths about their own commitments and about their own marriage.

Serving others may not seem like a romantic aspect of their marriage; and it certainly is not romantic if one thinks of soft music, dancing, candy, and flowers as the essence of romance. But marital love is much more substantive than romantic feelings. Such love includes practical ministry—two hearts beating as one in Christ's service. Charles and Susie's benevolence toward others is a reflection of their love for Christ and for one another. Had Charles and Susie not loved one another so well and supported one another wholeheartedly, they would not have been able to stretch their hands as they did to relieve the sufferings of others.

Christian compassion, for Charles and Susie, meant, in part, that they worked to cultivate a warm, welcoming, and attractive atmosphere at home. And this they did joyfully. Home was base for their larger ministry and the starting point of all that was good in their service to others.

A reporter for the *Sheffield Weekly Telegraph* reported in 1889 that Mrs. Spurgeon was significantly involved in "the work of the Tabernacle." The reporter referred to her as "a ministering angel among the poor in London" and "one of the most popular women in the big city."[18] Because she was an invalid at the time, Susie's ministry at the Tabernacle, as well as another church closer to her home, did not involve her physical presence but her support in other ways from her home.

In his biography, Danzy Sheen described Charles and Susie's solicitude:

> Mr. and Mrs. Spurgeon encouraged each other in such
> Christly deeds as the following:--A Baptist minister with
> a small income was ordered by the doctor to send his
> wife to the sea-side, as her only chance of convalescence
> after a long illness. It would cost £10. He had not such a
> sum in the world. He was in great distress of mind, when
> a letter reached him from Mr. Spurgeon, saying in the
> kindest way, "Would £10 be of any service to you now? If
> so, I shall be glad to send it to you." Imagine what tearful
> eyes, and overflowing heart, the minister wrote stating
> the above fact. The £10 was sent, and the sick wife and
> mother had a chance of recovery.[19]

Charles believed that the spiritual leader was "born on purpose to care for other people" and that he was then restless "until it [his heart] is full of such care."[20] For Charles *and* Susie, their greatest concern was for sinners to come to know the Savior. Charles wrote, "If we would save our hearers from the wrath to come, we must realize that they are our brothers. We must have sympathy with them, and anxiety about them; in a word, passion and compassion. May God grant these to us!"[21]

Susie recognized Charles's heart for godly philanthropy and how deeply he sympathized with the miseries of sufferers. He fervently prayed for the downtrodden. Susie said, "His heart was so big, it had room for others' griefs; and it was so full of love and pity, that he had always some to spare for those who needed it."[22]

Whether it was Susie choosing and packing books for poor pastors in her bookroom at Westwood or Charles preaching the gospel multiple times each week, or both of them caring for widows and orphans, it was from their love for God and one another that their service to others sprung.

A. Cunningham Burley had a unique insight into the Spurgeon family through his friendship with Charles Jr. He described Charles and Susie as "two gracious souls" who sympathized with each other's sufferings. He remembered them together "in unselfish and sacrificial sympathy during initial illness and weary weeks of prostration and infirmity."[23] Susie remembered,

> For ten blessed years I was permitted to encircle him
> with all the comforting care and tender affection it was
> a wife's power to bestow. Afterwards, God ordered it
> otherwise. He saw fit to reverse our position to each
> other; and for a long season, suffering instead of service
> became my daily portion, and the care of comforting sick
> wife fell upon my beloved.[24]

One effect of Charles and Susie's attentiveness was that it inspired others and also served as a powerful example to their grandchildren. Susie recollected in her book *Ten Years of My Life in the Service of the Book Fund* a warm story from New Year's Day at Westwood that illustrates how her life inspired her son and his children.

A tiny square box had arrived in the mail, addressed in her son Charles's handwriting. Her curiosity rose as she opened the box, and she was delighted to find "a pretty little, sovereign purse, with one of those satisfactory coins inside, and a morsel of paper with a memorandum to the following effect:—

'A New Year's Gift to dear Grandmama's Book Fund
From Susie and Dora.'"

Susie was thrilled. "It is a new and very amusing experience to have my son's little ones helping in my life-work!" Though they were young and lacked understanding as to the work that their Grandmama was doing through the Book Fund, Susie felt that the gift promised "well for future training and for bringing them up in the way they should go." *Who could tell?* she wondered. Perhaps in the future, they would take up her work "and carry it on more extensively, and not less lovingly," than she had done.[25]

The gift provoked Susie to reflect on her own sons' childhood. Embracing her role as a Grandmama, she desired to "be as wise and tender a *grandmother* as the Lord would have me be."[26]

Of Charles and Susie's relationship, Burley reflected, "It was just a wonderful life of perfect comradeship which neither affliction could cloud nor adversity conquer. Without the slightest taint of flattery Spurgeon could say sincerely of his good partner in compassion:

Teacher, tender comrade, wife,
A fellow-farer true through life,
Heart-whole and soul-free,
The Heavenly Father
Gave to me."[27]
(Poem by Robert Louis Stevenson)

CHAPTER 10

DAMP, COLD, AND FOGGY LONDON WINTERS exacerbated Charles's health problems. There was only one solution for him during the winter months from 1872–1892: depart the city for the "Sunny South"—Mentone, on the French Riviera. Yet, each time his horses neighed as they pulled his carriage away from his home, his heart sank, and his emotions were stirred, for he was leaving the one "dear as life" to him sequestered behind the doors of Westwood. Charles felt the tension of his suffering wife left behind to endure the cold London winters without him; but she urged him to follow their doctor's orders. She wanted more than anything for Charles's overtaxed mind and broken-down body to be relieved and restored, and if a journey to the coast would help, Susie was on board.

Her ailments were of such a nature that travel was impossible for her. They saw no other options—Susie couldn't travel without great risk to her health and Charles couldn't stay without endangering his. Susie was ably served by the household staff who met her every need—except one—her need for her husband. Charles always traveled with associates and over the years had developed numerous friendships at Mentone, yet—he longed for his best friend, Susie.

One of Charles and Susie's doctors was James Henry Bennet. He was a frequent traveler to Mentone, seeking healing for his own frail health. At one point he was near death and felt that he was miraculously healed beneath Mentone's almost perfect climate. It was his influence that led Charles to Mentone, a place that Bennet described as the most "picturesque spot" of the Riviera "encircled by its amphitheater of mountains."

LOVE'S REFLECTION

Charles and Susie never lost the wonder, the joy, and the sheer happiness of being in love—a happiness that they maintained for all of their thirty-six-year marriage. Perhaps they often looked back to that December day in 1855 when they were anticipating their wedding day and they would be formally united, making legal, official, and public the union that was already solidified in their hearts.

Susie had kept the December 1855 letter from Charles that he had written on his way to visit his parents for Christmas in Colchester. She sometimes lifted it from its envelope so that she could again read the sweet words of her young fiancé.

> Sweet One,--
>
> How I love you! I long to see you; and yet it is but half-an-hour since I left you. Comfort yourself in my absence by the thought that my heart is with you. My own gracious God bless you in all things,--in heart, in

feeling, in life, in death, in Heaven! May your virtues be perfected, your prospects realized, your zeal continued, your love to Him increased, and your knowledge of Him rendered deeper, higher, broader,--in fact, may more than even *my heart* can wish, or *my* hope anticipate, be yours for ever! May we be mutual blessings;--wherein I shall err, you will pardon; and wherein you may mistake, I will more than overlook.

Yours, till Heaven, and *then*,--

C.H. S.[1]

The first sentences of Charles and Susie's love story had been written on June 10, 1854, at the Crystal Palace and the last line of their earthly romance was January 31, 1892. Between those dates were years of joy, *and then*. The *and then* anticipated, what both Charles and Susie often referred to in their writings—their expectation of continuing their love for one another as they worshiped God in heaven. But first, there had to be a sad separation where one of the two lovers departed first in death.

THE LAST LOVE-LETTERS OF SPURGEON

The last published love letters from Charles to Susie were from 1890 until February 1891. For much of the rest of 1891, Charles was at home with Susie. When he was away, his letters came on schedule and brimmed with descriptive details of his surroundings, his experiences, his happiness, his afflictions, and his affections for God and for Susie.

After Charles's death, Susie wrote that she "reluctantly lifted from their [the letters] hiding-place, and re-read [them] with unspeakable love and sorrow." She remembered them as "full of brightness, and the fragrance of a deep and abiding affection; and filled with every detail concerning my beloved and his doings which could be precious to the heart of a loving wife."[2] Wherever Charles traveled, Susie was confident that his "loving heart" was home with her.[3] Charles told her as much, every day with a fresh letter or card. On days in which he was too ill to write, he dictated a message to his long-time secretary Harrald who mailed it to Susie.[4] Each letter delivered hope to Susie and stirred memories of happier times when she and Charles had almost effortlessly traveled the Continent together—Rome, Venice, Geneva, Paris, and more.

Reading Charles's last letters to Susie provides a picture of her aging husband, chock-full of challenges, yet writing Susie with the same freshness and interest he employed in his first correspondences to her from 1854. Susie includes several of his last letters in *C. H. Spurgeon's Autobiography*. They were written from the Riviera in late 1890 through February 5, 1891. By October of 1891, Charles was back in Mentone, and, as Susie recalled, "God gratified his longing,—cherished for years,—to have me with him [October 1891–January 1892]." Thrilled by having Susie at his side, Charles fully expected that they would return to London together in late winter. However, it was not to be. Susie, quoting from Naomi's words in the book of Ruth, wrote, "I went out full, and the Lord brought me home again empty; for after enjoying three months of exceeding sweetness, I unexpectedly found that I had gone to Mentone to see my beloved die!"[5]

But first there were his final letters to Susie *before* she traveled to Mentone with him.

Charles described the circumstances of his villa on the coast to Susie and included *"room for you."*[6] His letters overflowed with vivid word-pictures of his surroundings that he knew would delight his "wifey." Yet even in beautiful Mentone—as near to Eden as one could get after the fall—gout still made frequent appearances, driving Spurgeon from the stunning scenery projected from the Maritime Alps and Mediterranean Sea back to his four walls and bed. Charles's afflictions caused Susie deep concern as she prayed back in London. Susie described Charles's letters as "very tender records of the sick-room experiences,-- every detail told, and every possible consolation offered" yet each such letter brought "a weary season of suspense for the loving heart a thousand miles distant, and the trial of absence was multiplied tenfold by the distress of anxiety."[7]

When Charles's pain was most intense, he cried out to his friend Harrald, "I wish I were at home! I must get home."[8]

His longings for Susie were both painful for her to read and yet sweet to her ears—painful because of his suffering, sweet because he wanted to be with her. Susie's lip quivered as she read Charles's words: "Could not love his darling more."[9] Such kindhearted expressions were sincerely and freely given.

Charles kept a positive attitude during his episodes of sickness. In one of his messages he was excited to complete a daily task most take for granted: "TO-DAY I DRESSED MYSELF! A childish glee is on me as I record that fact."[10]

Other instances included his response to a happy note from Susie, "You write so sweetly. Yours is a hand which sets to music all it writes to me."[11] Regarding the beauty of Mentone and his ability to work again, Charles was exuberant, "This place is delicious. It is just 8 a.m., and I have both windows open, and I am writing to the low soft cadence of a rippling sea. Oh, that you were here."[12]

"Oh, that you were here," was the refrain of Charles in his messages home. He thought of Susie stuck in the severe London winter. "I wish I could think of something to cast a gleam of sunlight over

'Westwood.' If my love were light, you would live in the sun. I shall send some roses to-morrow, and they will prophesy of better days."[13] Every letter brought a measure of happiness to Susie; sometimes flowers were included with the dispatches. He wished to send Susie "a brazier of the coals of my heart, which have a most vehement flame."[14]

During a cold spell in Mentone, the sun broke through long enough to warm things up sufficient for Charles to take a ride. He couldn't wait to write Susie to tell her that her "Prince Charlie went forth in his chariot" enjoying everything that he saw, heard, and smelled. However only one thing would make his joyous day happier: "I want someone to show these things to,--and there is only one 'someone' who would fulfill my ideal."[15]

On New Year's Day 1891, Charles's letter left for Westwood with a greeting wishing Susie a happy New Year. She was his "sweetest and best."[16] He had been for a "drive in the delicious summer sunshine." Yet he wrote, "Oh, that you had been at my side."[17] His desire for Susie had an intoxicating effect on her heart—how could she not smile knowing that she was so loved by such a charming and expressive husband?

Susie kept herself busy during late 1890 and early 1891 by ministering to the needy of Thornton Heath near Westwood and by maintaining her Book Fund. The especially fierce winter that year depleted the scant resources of the poor, and Susie aided them by ensuring coal was delivered to their homes.[18] She also opened a soup kitchen that served the hungry daily. Charles sent money to support Susie's relief effort. Though Susie was not able to do the physical work of delivering coal or serving soup, she was the brains and the energy behind the work; and she was the careful overseer of her staff and other volunteers who performed the physical labor.

On good days, Charles drove around Mentone, afterwards returning quickly to his room to work on a book that he was writing or to edit a sermon. Sometimes he chose the shade of an olive tree near his hotel as a writing retreat. And at other times, he climbed the steep hill to the Mentone cemetery that offered a commanding view of the town and the deep blue Mediterranean Sea below with the Maritime Alps to his back. His daily drives helped him to maintain a healthy outlook as Mentone's landscape of flowers, plants, and trees teemed with color and scents, flourishing even in the winter months. After a particular two-mile walk, Charles offered a delightful message to Susie, "The sun, the air, the sea, all ministered to me; and I ministered to the Lord in grateful praise."[19] His health was improving. Hope returned.

Charles's last ever communication from Mentone to Susie was a postcard, and every word was classic Spurgeon.

> Mine Own,
>
> I telegraphed you to-day, and I hope your anxiety has ceased. There! At this moment, a mosquito popped on my nose, and Harrald has killed him! So may all your fears end! I am very much better; indeed well . . . . I am writing notes of "Good-bye" to friends. I hope soon to follow where this card is going; how delighted I am with the prospect! If you don't hear again, do not wonder; if anything should be wrong, I will wire at once. I am already with you in spirit. My heart has never left you. Blessed be God that we are spared to each other![20]

The card was dated Monday, February 2, 1891; Charles was preaching in London six days later on February 8. He had worked while he rested at Mentone, and now after a long journey home, he was back to work again. He was ready to restart his ministry with vigor; however, his infusion of energy was short-lived.

LAST DAYS IN LONDON
AND A VISIT TO STAMBOURNE

On May 17, Charles preached a sermon at the Metropolitan Tabernacle that, in hindsight, seems prophetic. His text was Psalm 31:15, "My times are in thy hand."

He trusted that God held him in His hands. His body was worn out, but his faith was strong. He proclaimed, "We assent to the statement, 'My times are in thy hand,' as to their result. Whatever is to come out of our life is in our heavenly Father's hand." Hopefully he declared, "The close of life is not decided by the sharp knife of the fates; but by the hand of love. We shall not die before our time, neither shall we be forgotten and left upon the stage too long."

Such a vision gave him courage to press on, even in the face of mountainous difficulties and duties. Charles longed for heaven: "The rougher the voyage the more the mariners long for port, and heaven becomes more and more a 'desired haven,' as our trials multiply."[21] Did Charles know that the desired haven was at hand? It was a haven that he anticipated very early in his London ministry when he wrote, "This life-journey is his [the Christian pilgrim's] one incessant occupation. He came into the world that he might march through it in haste. He is ever a pilgrim, in the fullest and truest sense."[22]

The first wave of troubled waters marking the beginning of the end of Spurgeon's life crashed the shore on May 18, the day after that sermon. He was gripped with pain and placed in his doctor's care. For three weeks, Charles stared death's cold gaze in the face. Yet, he rallied. On June 7, the hopes of Charles, Susie, church members, and Christians encircling the globe were raised when Charles regained strength to preach again to his congregation. However, it turned out to be another fleeting recovery. June 7, 1891, was the last time that Charles Haddon Spurgeon stepped foot in the Metropolitan Tabernacle—the last time that his familiar voice roared from his pulpit—the last time that his congregation heard their beloved pastor extoll the glory of Christ.

A Nostalgic Journey

Charles had long wanted to make a return visit to his grandfather's land in Stambourne. The green fields, rural paths, and the old parsonage and meeting house held memories sweet to his soul. He left on the sixty-mile journey on June 8, and he had a photographer join him to take a number of stills of the area for his upcoming book, *Memories of Stambourne.*[23] As he retraced his youthful footsteps, he visited old haunts connected to the formative years of his life. His mind raced to the upstairs room in his grandparents' home where he was first introduced to the sight, smell, and contents of the aforementioned old books. Likely, it was through Bunyan's allegory, read at Stambourne during Charles's childhood, that a picturesque image of heaven entered his mind.

Spurgeon's trip down memory lane painfully ended due to his contracting a throbbing headache. He was forced back home on Friday, June 12, where for three months he was mostly bedridden, dwelling somewhere between life and death.[24] Susie remembered that period as "a terrible time of suffering and suspense" and a time "when his precious life trembled in the balance, and it seemed as if the Master's call to His faithful servant might sound through the house at any moment." Susie set aside her work with the Book Fund to attend to her beloved's needs. She said, "He needed so constantly my personal care and love, that not much of my usual work could be accomplished."[25] Those three months were sweetened by cablegrams, telegrams, and letters assuring Susie and Charles of prayers for his recovery. Letters were received from leaders of the Church of England, nonconformist pastors, and spokesmen from every denomination, and political leaders such as William Gladstone. Even some of his theological opponents' hearts were warmed toward Spurgeon as they recognized the gravity of his situation and realized anew the greatness of the man.

Observing the outpouring of love that he and Susie received from leaders in the Church of England was especially moving to Charles. Early in his London ministry, he had preached a sermon, his most famous, entitled "Baptismal Regeneration," in which he vehemently attacked the church's doctrine of baptism. Though his convictions remained, love had grown between Charles and many evangelicals amongst the Church's leaders. Arguably, he was more regarded in evangelical corners of the Church of England than he was, at this time, by some pastors in the Baptist Union.

Spurgeon later reflected on the year 1891 and the love he had received from Christians around the world:

> During the past year I have been made to see that there is more love and unity among God's people than is generally believed. I speak not egotistically, but gratefully. I had no idea that Christian people, of every church, would spontaneously and importunately plead for the prolonging of my life. I feel myself a debtor to all God's people on this earth. Each section of the church seemed to vie with all the rest in sending words of comfort to my wife, and in presenting intercession to God on my behalf. If anyone had prophesied, twenty years ago, that

a dissenting minister, and a very outspoken one, too, would be prayed for in many parish churches, and in Westminster Abbey and St. Paul's Cathedral, it would not have been believed; but it was so. There is more love in the hearts of Christian people than they know of themselves. We mistake our divergences of judgment for differences of heart; but they are far from being the same thing. In these days of infidel criticism, believers of all sorts will be driven into sincere unity. . . . Between rationalism and faith there is an abyss immeasurable; but where there is faith in the Everlasting Father, faith in the Great Sacrifice, and faith in the Indwelling Spirit, there is a living, loving, lasting union.[26]

TO MENTONE WITH SUSIE:
A DREAM COME TRUE

On October 26, Charles *and* Susie and a small entourage began the long journey from London to Mentone via horse and carriage, train, and boat. Charles had long dreamt of Susie making the journey with him. His dream had seemed just that—a dream; however, this time, it was a dream come true.

Charles said of Mentone and the French Riviera that it was to him like "thy land, O Immanuel."[27] Susie wrote of Charles's happiness in bringing her to his beloved Mentone and sharing its beauty with her.[28] It almost defied belief to Charles that his "doubly dear Susie" was with him at the Rivera—the place that meant so much to him. For the first time ever, Charles was able to experience fullness of joy in his happy place with the woman that he loved more than life itself. "Oh, that you were here" had been his constant refrain—and now, she was there with Charles.

Susie described those days at Mentone as "glorious." "Never shall I cease to bless God for His tender mercy in permitting me to be with my beloved, and to minister to his happiness and comfort during those three blessed months. How full of joy they were to us both!"[29] Charles's health improved so much that Susie said she hoped "to keep my treasure for many long days to come."[30]

On December 31, Charles led a worship service at his hotel, the Beau Rivage. He encouraged his small congregation there to remember God's mercies to them in thanksgiving. In spite of his trying year, he confidently exclaimed, "God has been specially good to me."[31]

The next day, January 1, 1892, Charles again led the group in a service. He voiced his thankfulness that the specifics of one's future circumstances are hidden from everyone but God. Susie later reflected, "If I could have seen what these years held for me there would have been bitterness in every joy, and heartache in every pleasure."[32]

Always a visionary, Charles saw the way ahead as "*a pathway made from the first of January 1892, to the first of January 1893.*"[33] His perspective of God's sovereignty undergirded his hope. He said that "not the falling of a sparrow, nor the losing of a hair" was left to chance. Such gave Spurgeon confidence to face the rest of his pilgrimage to the Celestial City. "We are not left to pass through life as though it were a lone wilderness, a place of dragons and owls, for Jesus says, 'I will not leave you comfortless; I will come to you.'"[34]

Susie leaned forward, hanging on Charles's words. However, she couldn't have imagined that before the midnight hour of the last day of that very month that she would be a widow, and that her "Prince Charlie" would be gone.

Mentone with Charles was thrilling for Susie. For almost twenty years, she had remained behind in London as Charles convalesced in Mentone—now a part of their early marriage seemed magically restored, days in which they had traveled freely together in good health. For a time, all of their trials—the controversies, the London winter, the burdens of a thousand ministry responsibilities—all seemed to disappear as the two aged lovers explored the mountains and coast in idyllic surroundings. Gone were the years of Charles's frequent absences when Susie was afraid at home without him. Many nights' sleep had evaded her and even the softest sound startled her. When their dog Punchie barked, she imagined robbers outside.

How foolish she had been, she thought.[35] God had helped her through those hard times. And now—she was with Charles beside the canvas of what seemed to her to be God's most splendid handiwork as she held the hand of God's most wonderful man. There, old anxieties passed away—almost forgotten.

Laughter was plentiful between the lovers during their three months of "perfect happiness," especially when Charles pulled some prank on his beloved wife. Susie recalled, "He was full of fun and child-like pleasure, hiding behind a door on the way down to the 'table d'hote', to surprise me, or hurrying to be first ready, so as to chide the laggards when the dinner bell rang."[36] Charles seemed to be twenty-two years old again enjoying the company of his twenty-five-year-old new bride. Their honeymoon seemed to replay before their eyes. They celebrated their thirty-sixth wedding anniversary on January 8. Had it really been thirty-six years since the two young lovers were married? The time had passed so swiftly.

Though Charles and Susie believed that recovery was at hand, Charles's thoughts were nevertheless on the weighty issues of *both* life *and* death. "While you have yet to deal with the business and duty of life, look to God for the grace which these require; and when life is ebbing out, and your only thought is about landing on the eternal shore, then look to God your Saviour for dying grace in dying moments."[37] Dying grace in dying moments is just what Charles and Susie needed. "We may expect an inrush of divine strength when human strength is failing, and a daily impartation of energy as daily need requires. There is a hospice on every pass over the Alps of life, and a bridge across every river of trial which crosses our way to the Celestial City."[38]

Much earlier in their marriage, Charles and Susie had crossed the Alps and climbed the heights of mountains crossing bridges that spanned deep valleys below.

> A well-defined pathway is visible, but it appears devious and wandering; sometimes skirting a mountain-top, whence one could catch glimpses of "the land that is very far off"; and, further on, descending into a valley shadowed by clouds and darkness. At one time, it runs along amidst steep places, and overhanging rocks; anon, it winds across an open plain, brilliant with the sunshine of goodness and mercy, and fanned by breezes which are wafted from the fields of Heaven. There are flowers of joy and loving growing all along the way, even in the dark places; and "trees of lign aloes."[39]

"When will you return home to London?" From October of 1891 friends often asked this question of Charles. His typical response was, "I shall be home in February."[40] Charles anticipated a February return to his home at Westwood and, soon after, a return to his pulpit at the Metropolitan Tabernacle. His many prior trips to Mentone had facilitated his recovery from his various ailments, and he expected the same again. However, this time only his lifeless body would return to London, but he *would* journey home to heaven just less than an hour before the first strike of the clock at midnight, ushering in February of 1892.[41]

Susie recalled, "Christmas came and went. There were happy days of friendly festivity, and tender times of prayer and praise. And all the while the beloved one seemed to be gaining strength, for he worked joyfully at his Commentary on Matthew, and even recommenced his years-long work of revising the weekly sermon."[42]

January began hopefully. On the first Sunday of the month, Susie played her favorite hymns on the piano from *Sacred Songs and Solos* by Ira Sankey, and Charles preached for the small group who had gathered for worship. On January 9, Charles did what he had done most weeks since 1855: he revised a sermon to be included in the Metropolitan Tabernacle.[43]

On January 10, nineteen people gathered with Charles for a time of worship. Though he usually preached to the masses, he was just as much at home—perhaps more so, when he was gathered with a small band of Christians singing praises to God—doubly true because of Susie's presence.

On January 17, Charles participated in his last worship service on earth. That Lord's Day service began with him calling the congregation to sing, "O Thou My Soul, Bless God the Lord." Joseph Harrald then prayed, and then the congregation sang. Spurgeon gave an exposition from Matthew 25:21–28. After prayer, Spurgeon announced the last hymn—the last hymn that he would ever announce on earth. The hymn, based on the writings of Samuel Rutherford, proved to be extraordinarily appropriate for the occasion.

> The sands of time are sinking,
> The dawn of heaven breaks,
> The summer morn I've sighed for,—
> The fair, sweet morn awakes.
> Dark, dark hath been the midnight,
> But dayspring is at hand,

And "glory, glory dwelleth
In Immanuel's land."[44]

On the evening of January 20, gout pulsated through Charles's hand, delivering crippling pain and forcing him to bed. He never rose up again.[45] Though he had moments of cognizance, the end was near. A few days prior to his death, he told his long-time secretary and friend Joseph Harrald, "My work is done." Around that same time, he looked upward and whispered, "Susie. . . . Oh, wifie, I have had such a blessed time with my Lord!"[46] Around the world, multiplied thousands prayed for his healing.

The dreaded hour came just minutes after the clock struck 11 p.m. On the Lord's Day, January 31, 1892, Charles Haddon Spurgeon, the "Prince of Preachers" and Susie's great lover took his last breath and entered into the Celestial City to be with the Saviour whom he loved.

Susie wrote,

> His "abundant entrance", the "Well done, good and faithful servant!" of the Master, the great throng of white-robed spirits, who welcomed him as the one who first led them to the Saviour, the admiring wondering angels, the radiant glory, the *surprise* of that midnight journey which ended at the throne of God; all this, and much more of blessed reality for him, has lifted our bowed heads, and enabled us to bless the Lord, even though he has taken from us so incomparable a friend and pastor. All that was choice, and generous, and Christ-like, seemed gathered together in his character, and lived out in his life. He was pre-eminently "the servant of all"; yet he served with such humility and wisdom, that, with him, to *serve* was to *reign*. All are feeling now the power he wielded over men's

hearts; and because a prince of God, and a leader of men, has passed away, "our houses are left unto us desolate." I must not attempt to speak of his worth; words would utterly fail me; but the tears of multitudes, all over the world, testify to the irreparable loss they have sustained.[47]

Susie expected to soon join Charles around the throne of God.

Susie said that Charles had gone to "his everlasting reward, and the hallelujahs of heaven must hush and rebuke the sobs and sighs of earth."[48] Her grief was mixed with joy and thankfulness. "Looking up, with tear-dimmed eyes, to the God and Father of our Lord Jesus Christ, we can say, 'Even so, Lord, for thou hast made him most blessed forever. Thou has made him exceeding glad with thy countenance.'"[49]

In Susie's book *Ten Years After!*, she included a poem from Longfellow in reference to Charles's death.

> All was ended now, the hope, and the fear, and the sorrow,
> All the aching of heart, the restless unsatisfied longing,
> All the dull, deep pain, and constant anguish of patience!
> And, as she pressed once more the lifeless head to her bosom,
> Meekly she bowed her own, and murmured, "Father, I thank Thee!"[50]

Susie's chest was heavy with grief. "Bear with me, dear friends, as I draw the veil of silence over my great grief, and mutely pass over a period in my history, so full of sacred and solemn remembrances, so heavily laden with a sorrow that came from God, and which only Heaven can heal."[51] Nevertheless she was confident that the "pearly gates opened that my beloved might pass into the excellent glory, there has been (for *his* sake) deep down in my heart a low undertone of joy in God, like the singing of the pebbles on a beach when the tide comes rolling in." Though a year after his death, her grief had diminished somewhat, she felt that her expressions of joy in the Lord were still too muted.[52]

One of Spurgeon's favorite hymns was "Come Thy Fount of Every Blessing." The small band of Spurgeon's friends on the train sung this song on their way with Charles to Mentone in October of 1891. The words of the hymn were again on the lips of those at the quickly planned memorial service at the Hotel Beau Rivage. Spurgeon's friend Robert Shindler said of the song, "What a new meaning has been given to the second verse:—

'Here I raise my Ebenezer;
Hither by thine help I'm come;
And I hope, by thy good pleasure,
Safely to arrive at home!'"

Soon after Charles died, Susie lifted her eyes to the sky and focused on the planets Jupiter and Venus. They seemed brighter than normal to her. Turning to Joseph Harrald, she said, "I wonder what [Charles] thinks of those planets now." With only a brief pause, Harrald replied, "If they are inhabited, he has asked the Lord to let him go, that he may preach the gospel there." "No doubt of it," Susie agreed, "for how often he said that, when he got to heaven, he would stand at the corner of one of the streets, and proclaim to the angels the old, old story of Jesus and his love!"[53]

The first memorial service for Spurgeon was held at Mentone at the Scotch Presbyterian Church. Floral wreaths, sent by friends, adorned the chapel. Susie chose to contribute palm branches in declaration of her faith that Charles was victoriously standing before the throne of God and proclaiming, "Salvation to our God which sitteth upon the throne and unto the Lamb."[54]

The minister proclaimed, "'Charles Haddon Spurgeon is dead,' many are saying to-day; nay, not dead, but entered on life more abundant. The chamber of suffering has been exchanged for the land where the inhabitant shall no more say, 'I am sick.' He has gone from us; but he sees the King in his beauty."[55]

"Seeing the King in his beauty" was the hope of both Charles and Susie. It was that eternal vision that was a means of steadying their marriage and comforting them in their trials. Susie said "the safest way to Heaven" is "one step at a time, clinging fast to the Father's guiding hand, and our eyes 'ever toward the Lord.'"[56]

Years after Charles's death, Susie reluctantly opened a small book that Charles had given to her some thirty-five years prior. It was a diary of three months of his spiritual experiences from 1850. When Susie cracked open the little volume, her hands were shaking, and she began to cry. Her gaze fell on words, so moving, written when her beloved was so young. She loved Charles with all of her heart and prayed to remember that "the past *is past*, and the struggles and sorrows of earth are forever forgotten in the ecstasies of eternal glory."[57]

．．．．．．．．．．．．．．．．．．．．．．．．．．

Charles's body was transported back to London where a week of memorial services was held before his funeral and graveside service. Susie remained behind at Mentone for another month—a time that proved to bring healing to her heart and renewed focus to her own ministry. In London, upwards of a hundred thousand people lined the tear-stained streets as Spurgeon's funeral train, two miles long, passed by. London wept—the world wept—Susie wept.

During the February 10 memorial service, a letter from Susie to the Metropolitan Tabernacle was read. In it she recounted the happiness that Charles had felt during his last three months at Mentone. Bravely she declared, "The future both to you and to me, may seem clouded and uncertain, we will trust, and not be afraid." She comforted herself and the church that Charles was with Jesus. "Oh, the bliss, the rapture, of seeing his Saviour's face! Oh, the welcome home which awaited him as he left this sad earth. Not for a moment do I wish him back, though he was dearer to me than tongue can tell."[58]

THE REUNION OF CHARLES AND SUSIE

Susie's death came eleven years later, October 22, 1903. Her final years brought mostly better health that allowed her to support the extension of her husband's legacy, write several books, provide significant help in planting a church, manage the Book Fund, and serve as a contributor to and co-editor of *C. H. Spurgeon's Autobiography.*

The widowed Susie often meditated on seeing Christ and going to heaven. Her vision of heaven and Charles's eternal state enabled her to press forward with her own work. She anticipated following Charles to heaven at the appointed time. "I will follow thee my husband. Undying love from 'the wife of thy youth.'"[59]

Though Charles's death had ended her earthly marriage, Susie said it could not cut off her love for Charles. Seven years after Charles's death, Susie gazed off to the horizon and imagined Charles in the days of his youth—so full of energy and promise he was, always laboring in the Master's service. With her own death in view, she said, "I am watching and waiting to see my loved one again,--not as he was forty years or even seven years ago, but as he will be when I am called to rejoin him through the avenue of grace, or at the coming of our Lord Jesus Christ with all His saints." She kept watching and waiting and longing for heaven.[60] Charles had been her "dearly beloved husband," her "most precious treasure." After he died, Susie said, "God took my treasure from me."[61]

He was always on her mind. Sometimes she laughed. Sometimes she cried. She continued what she perceived her Savior and her husband would want her to do—to keep on serving Christ through the Book Fund. And she did just that to the joy and relief of many dear servants of God.

Susie's first biographer, Charles Ray, said that she contracted pneumonia in the summer of 1903 that lingered on until her death in October.[62] Susie was comforted by the regular visits of her sons, Thomas and Charles, along with her long-time friend and assistant, Elizabeth Thorne. Susie died on Thursday, October 22, 1903, and her body was laid beside Charles's in the same tomb atop the West Norwood Cemetery.

For Charles and Susie, their earthly sorrows were over and their perfected joys in the Lord and with one another began. There was no more slowness of step, nor coughing, faintness, or swollen fingers or ankles. Theological battles were ended—London's fog was lifted and joys eternal descended.

An eternal vision, like a giant magnet, pulled Charles and Susie forward through life's challenges. Though Susie was separated for eleven years after Charles's death, she said that she still loved him with all of her heart. After the days of their painful separation had ended, Charles's and Susie were reunited with a love supremely deeper than anything that they had experienced when married. *Yours, till Heaven* is only part of their love story. Now they are experiencing *and then*. For us, we can look back to Charles and Susie's marriage and learn from their example. We should also embrace their eternal vision of fellowship with Jesus and His saints. Such saints include Charles and Susie Spurgeon. We shall see *HIM*, that's the ultimate joy of Heaven, and we shall join *them* around the throne of God.

EPILOGUE

THOMAS SPURGEON STOOD INSIDE of the Primitive Methodist Chapel in Colchester to view the newly inscribed tablet hanging on the wall near the spot where his late father Charles had first trusted in Christ.[1] Thomas was very familiar with the story of that blustery snowy morning on January 6, 1850, when his father was converted after hearing a lay Methodist preacher's sermon from Isaiah 45:22.

Thomas recounted his Colchester visit to the congregation of the Metropolitan Tabernacle, where he had become pastor after his father Charles:

> I stood the week before last with uncovered head and throbbing heart, as near as it was possible to get to the spot where my dear father, your late beloved pastor, "looked and lived." I paid a special visit . . . to see the place where the local preacher cried, . . . "Look to Jesus. Young man, look to Jesus, look and live."[2]

Thomas urged his congregation to see the inscribed tablet for themselves: "Run and see it if you have opportunity, and as you look up at it, lift up your heart to God that you may be kept looking to Jesus."[3]

Two years after Charles's conversion, twenty-year old Susie Thompson was awakened to faith in Christ from an exposition of Romans, chapter 10, at the Poultry Chapel in London. No tablet marks the place of Susie's conversion, and the chapel no longer exists, but her experience was eternally *and* temporally significant.

Charles's and Susie's conversions provided the commonality necessary for their meeting, engagement, and marriage. Their marriage was because of the gospel; it was a marriage that was for the gospel, and it was a marriage that wonderfully displayed the gospel as it looked forward to heaven.

LOOKING BACK

Retracing the footsteps of his father had motivated Thomas to follow in them. He stood behind the Tabernacle pulpit and exhorted the multitude—many whom had come to Christ beneath his father's ministry—to look to Christ.

Are we not similarly encouraged when we go to the gravesites of loved ones and the monuments of great historical figures? We are looking for something when we visit such sacred places and recount the stories of history—something that calms our minds, stirs our emotions, awakens our affections, and changes us in positive ways. Charles and Susie's marriage can help us to look back on God's grace in former days, to look upward for God's help in the present, and to look forward to heaven where God's beauty is wonderfully displayed.

Our journey to get a closer view of Charles and Susie's marriage led us on a thousand-mile journey from London to Mentone. Their budding romance captured our attention at the Crystal Palace. We worshiped with them at the Metropolitan Tabernacle. Their homes at New Kent Road, Nightingale Lane, and Westwood refreshed us as we were invited inside, so full of hospitality and a love for others and for God. We joined them in Charles's study for family worship, and we heard his earnest prayers. We sang around the piano as Susie played from Ira Sankey's *Sacred Songs*. We sympathized with Charles and Susie as they suffered, and we cheered them onward when they battled against discouragement and doubt. We read their tender love letters and were moved by their romantic expressiveness to follow their example. We got a sense of their place and mission as they traversed through Victorian England and invested in gospel-driven benevolent enterprises. We laughed at their humor, admired their creativity, learned from their teamwork, and pondered their eternal vision. We smiled as they delighted in one another at Mentone and wept as Susie stood courageously there at the deathbed of Charles. And, we witnessed Susie's fierce love for Charles during the remaining eleven years of her life.

When Susie died on October 22, 1903, she joined Charles in eternal bliss. The gospel brought Charles to London and Susie to Charles—and the gospel brought both to the place that they longed for, Immanuel's Land, where their love was perfected.

WALKING WITH HEROES

How they loved one another: Charles said, "If there is only one good wife in England, I am the man who put the ring on her finger, and long may she wear it. God bless the dear soul if she can put up with me; she shall never be put down by me."[4] Charles and Susie, faith heroes from history, left behind for us an exemplary marriage. We shrink back from worshiping godly heroes for good reason—they were, like we are, frail and fallen. However, they are now what we shall be—perfected in heaven. Though we refuse idolatrous reverence, we unhesitatingly look to Charles and Susie's marriage as a godly example for our own relationships.

Yours: Charles said that a husband is to "lavish [love] upon his wife" that "he must give to nobody else in the world."[5] A happy marriage is secured in the commitment that "yours" entails.

Till: The space between August 2, 1854, when Charles asked and Susie accepted his proposal of marriage and 11:05 p.m., January 31, 1892, when he died and was received into heaven. *Till* was their thirty-six-year praiseworthy marriage that filled the gap between "I do" and death.

Heaven: Charles and Susie's destination. Like Bunyan described, they were two pilgrims on a journey to the Celestial City.

Charles's pledge, "Yours, till Heaven," included two additional words, *and then.* He fully expected to know and love Susie in heaven.

> I have heard of a good woman, who asked her husband, when she was dying, "My dear, do you think you will know me when you and I get to heaven?" "Shall I know you?" he said, "why, I have always known you while I have been here, and do you think I shall be a greater fool when I get to heaven?" I think it was a very good answer. If we have known one another here, we shall know one another there.[6]

Charles and Susie's heavenly love is not marital love—it is vastly superior. The apostle Paul wrote in Philippians 1:3 that being with Christ is "far better" than anything (including marriage) that one enjoys during his earthly life. Though *not* married *to* one another in heaven, Charles and Susie *are* united to Jesus.

> Death must sever the conjugal tie between the most loving mortals, but it cannot divide the links of this immortal marriage. In heaven they marry not, but are as the angels of God; yet there is this one marvelous exception to the rule, for in Heaven Christ and His Church shall celebrate their joyous nuptials. This affinity, as it is more lasting, so is it more near than earthly wedlock.[7]

It was their anticipation of heaven's marriage, with its perpetual joy, that compelled Charles and Susie to love one another well in their marriage.

Charles and Susie's love story lives on—helping us to dig beneath trivial romantic fancies into the very heart of a loving marriage.

When Charles died, Susie remained for a month in Mentone— she was too frail to join in the week of London memorials honoring the great preacher. While the children wept at the orphanages; students of his college steeled their resolve; old friends paid their tributes; and messages were delivered from around the world—Susie walked the steps that Charles had often traversed when at Mentone—steps that he led Susie through during their three months together there. She recalled his stories, his descriptive letters home about the shores of the Mediterranean, and how he longed for her presence.

Susie's last months with Charles were like her first with him— laughter, happiness, and anticipation. She remembered each site that he had pointed out to her, and she followed Charles's footsteps all the way down to the shore of the bright blue Mediterranean where she pondered:

Down by the sea-shore, with the clear blue waters
kissing the shingle at my feet, and making even the
stones to sing a constant song of joy, I used to sit and
think of my beloved's eternal bliss, till I could almost
join in the universal melody around me, though the
tears were blinding my eyes, and my heart ached with
unspeakable grief. I could not see to the other side of the
bright Mediterranean waters, the light was too dazzling,
and my vision was bounded; but I knew that, beyond
the horizon, there lay a summer land, where the rigours
of winter are unknown, and the icy winds of the North
never blow. Even so, I could not with my bodily eyes
see to the other shore of that separating sea which my
precious husband had so lately crossed; but faith *knew*
the Celestial City was there, and that he was even then
walking the golden streets, rejoicing in the fullness of
joy at God's right hand. Better, ay, far better, to be with
Christ, than to be with me.[8]

Susie said that her love for Charles grew stronger and that its spiritual fulfillment would be realized, "when we shall meet in the glory-land and worship together before the throne."[9]

Charles had assured her those many years before that he was, "Yours, till Heaven." For thirty-six years Susie found that his promise was true. From Mentone's peaceful shores she looked across the sea anticipating meeting him in the glory-land. And, she did.

Charles and Susie's steps are left for us to follow.

Married Love

TO MY WIFE.

Over the space which parts us, my wife,
I'll cast me a bridge of song,
Our hearts shall meet, O joy of my life,
On its arch unseen but strong.

E'en as the stream forgets not the sea,
But hastes to the ocean's breast,
My constant soul flows onward to thee
And finds in thy love its rest.

The swallows must plume their wings to greet
New summers in lands afar;
But dwelling at home with thee I meet
No winter my year to mar.

The wooer his new love's name may wear
Engraved on a precious stone;
But in my heart thine image I wear,
That heart has been long thine own.

The glowing colours on surface laid,
Wash out in a shower of rain,
Thou need'st not be of rivers afraid,
For my love is dyed ingrain.

And as ev'ry drop of Garda's lake
Is tinged with the sapphire's blue;
So all the powers of my mind partake
Of joy at the thought of you.

The glittering dewdrops of dawning love
Exhale as the day grows old,
And fondness, taking the wings of a dove,
Is gone like a tale of old;

But mine for thee from the chambers of joy,
With strength came forth as the sun,
Nor life nor death shall its force destroy,
Forever its course shall run.

All earthborn love must sleep in the grave,
To its native dust return;
What God hath kindled shall death outbrave
And in heav'n itself shall burn.

Beyond and above the wedlock tie
Our union to Christ we feel,
Uniting bonds which were made on high
Shall hold us when earth shall reel.

Though he who chose us all worlds before,
Must *reign* in our hearts alone,
We fondly believe that we shall adore,
Together before his throne.

Hull, Sep. 1865.   C. H. Spurgeon[10]

Acknowledgments

SPURGEON REFERRED TO HIS LONGTIME ASSISTANT J. W. Harrald as his "Armor-Bearer." During his last three months of life, Spurgeon worked to complete his commentary on Matthew, *The Gospel of the Kingdom*. Before he finished the last section, he died; Harrald was at his side. The "Armor Bearer" pieced together sections from Spurgeon's previous writings/sermons on Matthew and completed the volume; Susie wrote the introduction. Some years later, Harrald and Susie coedited the four volume *C. H. Spurgeon's Autobiography*. Though an interesting biography could be written about Harrald, he was content to serve his friend and fellow minister in relative obscurity. It struck me recently that, though Spurgeon was brilliant, creative, and productive on his own, he could never have accomplished what he did without his supportive wife and his ministry team. Part of the secret of Spurgeon's almost unbelievable productivity is found in his assistants.

Though I do not have the abilities of Spurgeon, nor the depth of his support system at my disposal, I nevertheless wrote this book in the context of a very exemplary community. Publishing a book requires teamwork, and this book is better due to the excellent team that shared ideas with me, held me accountable, encouraged me when I was down, and assisted me in a thousand other ways.

I am thankful that Moody Publishers (MP) published both *Susie: The Life and Legacy of Susannah Spurgeon* and *Yours, till Heaven:*

The Untold Love Story of Charles and Susie Spurgeon. This latest project was my first with acquisitions editor Amy Simpson. Amy believed in my book idea early on, and she faithfully shepherded this project from proposal, to contract, to completion. Thanks, Amy! This is my second book with developmental editor Amanda Cleary Eastep. After many email and phone conversations through two books now, Amanda is like a member of the Rhodes family. My wife, Lori, is very thankful that Amanda helped to calm my anxious brain when I was distressed about the book and our youngest daughter, Abigail, really likes "Miss Amanda." Amanda, thank you for your off-the-charts excellent editing and for your friendship.

To the rest of the Moody team: Thank you! Randall Payleitner, associate publisher, who opened the front door for me to write for MP; Ashley Torres, for your excellent marketing expertise; Erik Peterson, for your fantastic creative directing; Connor Sterchi, for your amazing ability to manage the process; Kevin Utecht, for your energetic work as publicist for this project; and for a great team of proofreaders, typesetters, and the rest of the Moody family! Charles and Susie would be delighted that the publisher who carries their friend D. L. Moody's name is helping to keep the Spurgeon legacy alive.

Thank you Jason K. Allen, president of Midwestern Baptist Theological Seminary (MBTS), for your generous foreword and for your love for all things Spurgeon. I am deeply honored that you were willing to add your name and words to this volume. MBTS is a top academic institution and the home of the beautiful Spurgeon Library that houses about six thousand volumes from Spurgeon's personal collection. Under Dr. Allen's extraordinary leadership, MBTS has enjoyed tremendous growth.

A special thank you to friends who assisted me in some important ways: Jessica Roberson, Scott and Bonney Williams, Kevin and

Kelly Jarrard, Andrew Neveils, Samuel Roys, William (Bill) and Maureen Gardner (our dear London assistants), Susie Spurgeon Cochrane (great-great granddaughter of Charles and Susie), Hilary Spurgeon, George Scondras, Eric James, Cory Pitts, David Bailey, Chris Reese, Brian Albert, Phillip Ort, Geoff Chang, Alex DiPrima, and many more. Your support bolstered me, and I am blessed to call you my friends.

I am much appreciative to the Christian leaders who endorsed this book—your thoughtful reading of the manuscript and your kind endorsements mean so much to me. Thank you for allowing your name to be included, for perpetuity, on *Yours, till Heaven*.

I owe a tremendous debt to the Southern Baptist Theological Seminary. Its leadership and faculty provided me a community that encourages research and writing. Thank you to my friends and mentors R. Albert Mohler Jr., Donald S. Whitney, Michael Haykin, Tom Nettles, Joe Harrod, Jeff Robinson, and Hershael York.

My best writing usually happens at one of my favorite retreat places, including the Legacy Hotel and Conference Center at the Southern Baptist Theological Seminary in Louisville, Kentucky (thanks great Legacy staff); Clear Creek Baptist Bible College in Pineville, Kentucky (thanks Donnie Fox and Michael DeLand); the Historic Brookstown Inn in Winston Salem, NC (special thanks to Aaron Backfield); Cavendar Creek Vineyards, Dahlonega, GA (thanks Dr. Claire Livingston); and Pinnacle Retreat Center in Clayton, GA (thanks Ed). All the places above are staffed with great folks who went out of their way to make sure I had all I needed for a great writing experience. I encourage you to visit one and to visit all.

Hannah Wyncoll (daughter of Peter Masters, longtime pastor of the Metropolitan Tabernacle [MT] in London) gave permission to use archival material from the MT; Pastor John Clevely of

Beulah Baptist Church in Thornton Heath, London, provided digital copies of church records connected to Charles and Susie; Melvyn Harrison, chairman, Crystal Palace Foundation, gave permission to use a number of photographs, and he engaged in excellent and helpful correspondence concerning the Crystal Palace. Pastor T. D. Hale generously provided an overwhelming number of photographs of Charles and Susie from his large Spurgeon collection of books, articles, and photographs. Emily Burgoyne, Angus Librarian, Regent's Park College, University of Oxford, provided her help with Susie and also communicated with me regarding this book.

Thanks to readers of *Susie: The Life and Legacy of Susannah Spurgeon* for your emails, social media correspondence, phone calls, and much encouragement to keep writing about Spurgeon. *Susie* surpassed all expectations and provided a foundation for this book, thanks to you!

Thanks to my mother, Dorothy, and my father- and mother-in-law, Rodney and Lou Webb, for their tremendous support and love.

Special thanks to Grace Community Church of North Georgia (GCC), who offered prayer support and encouragement, and who viewed my writing as an extension of my ministry. I am blessed and thankful to serve a sweet and supportive congregation.

To my lovely wife, Lori, and our six daughters, Rachel, Hannah, Sarah, Mary, Lydia, and Abigail; sons-in-law, Adrian and Caleb; and five grandchildren—Susannah, Josiah, Caleb, Eden Rose, and Owen—you have sacrificed much and encouraged me often as I have worked on this book.

Soli Deo gloria: to God alone be glory!

Notes

INTRODUCTION

1. C. H. Spurgeon, *C.H. Spurgeon's Autobiography: Compiled from His Diary, Letters, and Records, by His Wife and His Private Secretary* (London: Passmore and Alabaster, 1897–1900), 2:26.
2. Richard Ellsworth Day, *The Shadow of the Broad Brim: The Life Story of Charles Haddon Spurgeon, Heir of the Puritans* (Philadelphia: The Judson Press, 1934), 106.
3. C. H. Spurgeon, *Autobiography*, 2:24. "Precious Love" is one of the terms of endearment that Charles used for Susie.
4. Ibid., 2:27.
5. C. H. Spurgeon, *Autobiography*, 3:186.
6. C. H. Spurgeon, *The Sword and the Trowel: A Record of Combat with Sin & Labor for the Lord* (London: Passmore & Alabaster, 1892), 139.
7. C. H. Spurgeon, *Autobiography*, 2:1.
8. Ibid.
9. Ibid.
10. George C. Lorimer, *Charles Haddon Spurgeon: The Puritan Preacher in The Nineteenth Century* (Boston: James H. Earle, Publisher, 1892), 142.
11. C. H. Spurgeon, *Autobiography*, 2:1.
12. Ibid.
13. C. H. Spurgeon, *Lectures to My Students* (London: Marshall, Morgan & Scott, 1954), 21.
14. C. H. Spurgeon, *The Sword and the Trowel* (1903), 551.
15. C. H. Spurgeon, *Autobiography*, 1:146.
16. C. H. Spurgeon, *Autobiography*, 2:1.
17. C. H. Spurgeon, *The Metropolitan Tabernacle Pulpit: Sermons Preached and Revised by C. H. Spurgeon* (Pasadena, TX: Pilgrim Publications, 1970–2006), 8:651.
18. Ibid., 654.
19. Ibid.

CHAPTER 1: A NOT SO VICTORIAN ROMANCE

1. Patricia Stallings Kruppa, *Charles Haddon Spurgeon: A Preacher's Progress* (New York: Garland Publishing, 1982), 107.
2. Ibid.

3. William Williams, *Charles Haddon Spurgeon: Personal Reminiscences*, revised and edited by his daughter Marguerite Williams (London: The Religious Tract Society, n.d.), 12.
4. H. I. Wayland, *Charles H. Spurgeon: His Faith and Works* (Philadelphia: American Baptist Publication Society, 1892), 7.
5. C. H. Spurgeon, *Autobiography*, 2:5.
6. C. H. Spurgeon, *Autobiography*, 2:7.
7. Ibid.
8. Daniel Pool, *What Jane Austen Ate and Charles Dickens Knew: From Fox Hunting to Whist—the Facts of Daily Life in 19ᵗʰ-Century England* (New York: Simon and Schuster, 1993), 264.
9. Christian T. George, ed., *The Lost Sermons of C. H. Spurgeon: His Earliest Outlines and Sermons Between 1851 and 1854* (Nashville: B&H Academic, 2016), 1:8.
10. Pool, *What Jane Austen Ate*, 31.
11. Ibid., 30.
12. Ibid.
13. Timothy Larsen, *A People of One Book: The Bible and the Victorians* (Oxford: Oxford University Press, 2011), 1.
14. Ibid., 2.
15. Ibid.
16. Ibid., 3.
17. Sally Mitchell, *Daily Life in Victorian England* (Westport, CT: The Greenwood Press, 1996), 157.
18. Ibid.
19. Ibid., 159.
20. Lewis Drummond, *Spurgeon: Prince of Preachers* (Grand Rapids: Kregel, 1992), 229.
21. C. H. Spurgeon, *Autobiography*, 2:177–78.
22. Ibid., 2:180.
23. Ibid.
24. Ibid., 2:182.
25. Mrs. C. H. Spurgeon, *Ten Years After!: A Sequel to "Ten Years of My Life in the Service of the Book Fund"* (London: Passmore & Alabaster, 1895), vi.

CHAPTER 2: BIBLICAL SPIRITUALITY

1. C. H. Spurgeon, *Autobiography*, 2:9.
2. Mrs. C. H. Spurgeon, *Ten Years After!*, 26.
3. C. H. Spurgeon, *Till He Come: Communion Meditations and Addresses* (London: Marshall Brothers, n.d.), 44.
4. C. H. Spurgeon, *Autobiography*, 2:24.
5. Ibid., 2:26.
6. W. Y. Fullerton, *Thomas Spurgeon: A Biography* (London: Hodder and Stoughton, n.d.), 41.
7. C. H. Spurgeon, *Autobiography*, 1:69.

8. J. C. Carlile, *C. H. Spurgeon: An Interpretative Biography* (London: The Religious Tract Society, 1933), 24.

9. See Isaiah 45:22. Spurgeon shared his testimony many times in his sermons and all biographies of Spurgeon tell the story.

10. C. H. Spurgeon, *The Letters of Charles Haddon Spurgeon* (London: Marshall Brothers, Limited, 1923), 13.

11. C. H. Spurgeon, *Letters*, 22.

12. *Susie: The Life and Legacy of Susannah Spurgeon* draws from census records and various other legal documents to shed some light on Susie's parents and her childhood. Ray Rhodes, *Susie: The Life and Legacy of Susannah Spurgeon* (Chicago: Moody, 2018).

13. Mrs. C. H. Spurgeon, *A Cluster of Camphire: Words of Cheer and Comfort to Sick and Sorrowful Souls* (London: Passmore & Alabaster, 1898; repr., Springfield, MO: Particular Baptist Press, 2016), 1.

14. Leland Ryken, *Worldly Saints: The Puritans as They Really Were* (Grand Rapids: Zondervan, 1986), 40.

15. Doreen Moore, *Good Christians Good Husbands? Leaving a Legacy in Marriage & Ministry* (Ross-shire, Scotland: Christian Focus Publications, 2004), 62.

16. Ibid., 64.

17. Ibid., 82.

18. Michael Reeves, *Spurgeon on the Christian Life: Alive in Christ* (Wheaton, IL: Crossway, 2018), 36. Quote is from a Spurgeon sermon.

19. C. H. Spurgeon, *The Metropolitan Tabernacle Pulpit*, 11:253.

20. Ibid., 257–58.

21. C. H. Spurgeon, *Autobiography*, 2:9.

22. Ibid., 2:10.

23. Mrs. C. H. Spurgeon, *Ten Years After!*, 38.

24. C. H. Spurgeon, *Spurgeon's Practical Wisdom or John Ploughman's Talk & John Ploughman's Pictures: Plain Advice for Plain People* (Edinburgh, reprint from 1869 &1880: The Banner of Truth Trust, 2009), 71.

25. Charles Ray, *The Life of Susannah Spurgeon, In Free Grace and Dying Love* (1903; repr., Edinburgh: The Banner of Truth Trust, 2013), 173.

26. C. H. Spurgeon, *The New Park Street Pulpit* (April 1856; repr., Pasadena, TX: Pilgrim, 1970–2006), 1:111.

27. Susannah Spurgeon, *Free Grace and Dying Love: Morning Devotions* (1896; repr., Edinburgh: The Banner of Truth Trust, 2013), 64.

28. C. H. Spurgeon, *The Metropolitan Tabernacle Pulpit*, 25:631.

29. Ibid.

30. C. H. Spurgeon, *The Sword and the Trowel* (1898), 50.

31. C. H. Spurgeon, *The Metropolitan Tabernacle Pulpit*, 25:629.

32. Ibid., 20:506.

33. Mrs. C. H. Spurgeon, *Ten Years After!*, 27.

34. Mrs. C. H. Spurgeon, *A Cluster of Camphire*, 40.

35. C. H. Spurgeon, *The Metropolitan Tabernacle Pulpit*, 20:506.

36. Ibid., 54:362.

37. Kenney Dickenson, "How to Experience God Like Spurgeon," October 19, 2017, https://www.spurgeon.org/resource-library/blog-entries/how-to-experience-god-like-spurgeon.

38. Susannah Spurgeon, *A Basket of Summer Fruit* (London: Passmore and Alabaster, 1901; repr., Forest, VA: Corner Pillar, 2010), 109.

39. Ibid., 111–12.

40. John Bunyan, *A Relation of The Holy War* (New York: W M. L, Allison, n.d.).

41. C. H. Spurgeon, *The Metropolitan Tabernacle Pulpit*, 20:506.

42. Ibid.

43. C. H. Spurgeon, *Autobiography*, 2:18.

44. Ibid.

45. Ibid., 2:19.

46. Ibid., 2:24.

47. Ibid., 2:26.

48. Ernest W. Bacon, *Spurgeon: Heir of the Puritans* (Grand Rapids: Eerdmans, 1968), 12–13.

49. C. H. Spurgeon, *The Interpreter: Scripture for Family Worship* (London: Passmore and Alabaster, n.d.), iii.

50. C. H. Spurgeon, *Autobiography*, 4:64.

51. Ibid., 4:4.

52. Walter E. Houghton, *The Victorian Frame of Mind* (London: Yale University Press, 1956), 341.

53. Henry D. Northrop, *The Life and Works of Charles Haddon Spurgeon* (1892; repr., Murfreesboro, TN: Sword of the Lord Publishers, 2004), 50.

54. Mrs. C. H. Spurgeon, *Ten Years After!*, 38.

55. Ibid., 65.

56. Russell H. Conwell, *The Life of Charles H. Spurgeon: The World's Great Preacher* (Philadelphia: Edgewood, 1892), 236.

CHAPTER 3: SHARED MISSION

1. Russell H. Conwell, *Life of Charles H. Spurgeon*, 233.

2. Ibid., 228.

3. Ibid., 233–34.

4. Geoff Chang, "Spurgeon's Church Planting Strategy," HistoricalTheology.org, October 26, 2018, https://www.historicaltheology.org/articles/2018/10/26/spurgeons-church-planting-strategy?rq=spurgeon/#more-783=.

5. G. Holden Pike, *The Life and Work of Charles Haddon Spurgeon*, 6 vols. (London: Cassell and Company, n.d.), 5:162–63.

6. C. H. Spurgeon, *The Sword and the Trowel* (1903), 551.

7. Robert Shindler, *The Life and Labors of Charles Haddon Spurgeon* (New York: A. C. Armstrong and Son, 1892), 201.

8. Charles Ray, *Mrs. C. H. Spurgeon* (1903; repr., Pasadena, TX: Pilgrim Publications, 1973), 3.

9. Quoted in Larry J. Michael, *Spurgeon on Leadership: Key Insights for Christian Leaders from the Prince of Preachers* (Grand Rapids: Kregel, 2010), 132.
10. C. H. Spurgeon, *Autobiography*, 3:183–84.
11. Frederick Dolman, "Mrs. Charles H. Spurgeon" in *The Ladies Home Journal*, vol. IX, no. 4 (Philadelphia: Curtis Publishing Co., March 1892), 3.
12. From the archives of Beulah Family Church in, Thornton Heath, London. During Charles and Susie's lifetime, the church was known as Beulah Baptist Church. Records made available by Pastor John Clevely.
13. C. H. Spurgeon, *The Sword and the Trowel* (1896), 218.
14. Mike Nicholls, *C. H. Spurgeon: The Pastor Evangelist* (Didcot, England: Oxford, 1992), 63.
15. Ibid., 55.
16. Ibid., 56.
17. J. C. Carlile, *An Interpretative Biography*, 19.
18. Mrs. C. H. Spurgeon, *Ten Years After!*, vi.
19. J. C. Carlile, *An Interpretative Biography*, 169.
20. C. H. Spurgeon, *Autobiography*, 2:183.
21. Ibid.
22. William Williams, *Personal Reminiscences*, 54.
23. C. H. Spurgeon, *Autobiography*, 2:183.
24. Ibid., 184.
25. Ibid.
26. William Williams, *Personal Reminiscences*, 55.
27. C. H. Spurgeon, *Autobiography*, 2:185.
28. Ibid.
29. Ibid.
30. C. H. Spurgeon, *Spurgeon's Practical Wisdom*, 71–72.
31. Ibid., 94–95.
32. Ibid., 95–96.
33. C. H. Spurgeon, *Autobiography*, 2:16.
34. Ibid., 2:17.
35. Mrs. C. H. Spurgeon, *Ten Years of My Life in the Service of the Book Fund* (London: Passmore and Alabaster, 1886), 33–34.
36. C. H. Spurgeon, *Autobiography*, 2:5.
37. Ibid., 2:6.
38. Ibid., 2:17.
39. Ibid., 2:16–17.
40. J. C. Carlile, *An Interpretative Biography*, 189.
41. Ernest W. Bacon, *Spurgeon: Heir of the Puritans*, 45.
42. Mrs. C. H. Spurgeon, *Ten Years of My Life*, 21.
43. Ibid., 45.
44. Ibid., 57.
45. Ibid.
46. Ibid., 3.
47. Ibid., 32.

CHAPTER 4: MUTUAL SUPPORT

1. C. H. Spurgeon, *Memories of Stambourne* (New York: American Tract Society, n.d.), iii.
2. C. H. Spurgeon, *Autobiography*, 1:3.
3. Charles Ray, *The Life of Susannah Spurgeon, in Free Grace and Dying Love*, 166.
4. C. H. Spurgeon, *The Metropolitan Tabernacle Pulpit*, 36:200.
5. C. H. Spurgeon, *The Saint and His Savior: The Progress of the Soul in the Knowledge of Jesus* (New York: Sheldon, Blakeman & Co., 1858), 340–41.
6. Ibid., 341.
7. Ibid.
8. C. H. Spurgeon, *Autobiography*, 2:196.
9. Ibid.
10. C. H. Spurgeon, *The Saint and His Saviour*, 342–43.
11. Quoted in Tom Nettles, *Living by Revealed Truth: The Life and Pastoral Theology of Charles Haddon Spurgeon* (Fearn, Ross-shire, Scotland: Christian Focus Publications, 2013), 598.
12. Charles Ray, *Mrs. C. H. Spurgeon* (1903; repr., Pasadena, TX: Pilgrim Publications, 1973), 2–3.
13. C. H. Spurgeon, *The Sword and the Trowel* (1892), 42.
14. C. H. Spurgeon, *Lectures to My Students* (1875–1894; repr., Edinburgh: The Banner of Truth Trust, 2008), 188.
15. Ibid., 179.
16. Kyle Lee Julius, (2018) "What's Wrong with Me?: How Spurgeon Battled Depression," https://www.desiringgod.org/articles/whats-wrong-with-me?fbclid=IwAR1V7TLbchx92I5Cg-WoDYc9icjC7Lrdt4R4DZYolVL8uQZl3iO0-xLOrsU.
17. Russell H. Conwell, *Life of Charles H. Spurgeon*, 228.
18. Mark Hopkins, *Nonconformity's Romantic Generation: Evangelical and Liberal Theologies in Victorian England* (Eugene, OR: Wiph and Stock, 2006), 130.
19. Ernest W. Bacon, *Spurgeon: Heir of the Puritans*, 45.
20. H. I. Wayland, *Charles H. Spurgeon: His Faith and Works*, 226.
21. Mrs. C. H. Spurgeon, *A Cluster of Camphire*, 42.
22. Ibid., 76–77.
23. C. H. Spurgeon, *The Cheque Book of the Bank of Faith* (New York: A. C. Armstrong & Son, 1892), v.
24. Ibid., vii.
25. Winston Churchill reportedly referred to depression as the "black dog."
26. William Brian Albert, "'When the Wind Blows Cold': The Spirituality of Suffering and Depression in the Life and Ministry of Charles Spurgeon" (PhD diss., The Southern Baptist Theological Seminary, 2015), 20.
27. Quoted in William Brian Albert, "'When the Wind Blows Cold,'" 20.
28. In *Susie: The Life and Legacy of Susannah Spurgeon*, it is surmised that Charles demonstrated characteristics in common with those diagnosed with PTSD.
29. Richard Ellsworth Day, *The Shadow of the Broad Brim*, 96.

30. Quoted in Patricia Stallings Kruppa, *Charles Haddon Spurgeon: A Preacher's Progress* (New York: Garland Publishing, 1982), 92.

31. Ibid., 93–94.

32. Staff, "21 Funniest Spurgeon Quotes," The Spurgeon Center, September 27, 2016, https://www.spurgeon.org/resource-library/blog-entries/21-funniest-spurgeon-quotes/.

33. Russell H. Conwell, *Life of Charles H. Spurgeon*, 235.

34. William Williams, *Personal Reminiscences*, 33.

35. Jesse Page, *Spurgeon: His Life and Ministry* (London: S. W. Partridge & Co., 1903), 148.

36. C. H. Spurgeon, *Autobiography*, 3:247.

37. Mark Hopkins, *Nonconformity's Romantic Generation*, 130.

38. Quoted in Tom Nettles, *Living by Revealed Truth*, 595.

39. Henry D. Northrop, *The Life and Works of Charles Haddon Spurgeon*, 61.

40. David W. Bebbington, *The Dominance of Evangelicalism: The Age of Spurgeon and Moody* (Downers Grove, IL: InterVarsity Press, 2005), 41.

41. D. G. Hart and R. Albert Mohler Jr., eds. *Theological Education in the Evangelical Tradition*, "Spurgeon and British Evangelical Theological Education," David W. Bebbington (Grand Rapids: Baker Books, 1996), 220.

42. Patricia Kruppa, *Charles Haddon Spurgeon*, 105.

43. Richard Ellsworth Day, *The Shadow of the Broad Brim*, 106–7.

44. Mrs. C. H. Spurgeon, *A Cluster of Camphire*, 39.

45. Mrs. C. H. Spurgeon, *Ten Years of My Life*, 71–72.

46. This was likely Elizabeth Thorne.

47. Mrs. C. H. Spurgeon, *Ten Years of My Life*, 72.

48. Ibid.

49. Mrs. C. H. Spurgeon, *A Cluster of Camphire*, 82.

50. C. H. Spurgeon, *The Saint and His Saviour*, 336.

51. Helmut Thielicke, *Encounter with Spurgeon* (Cambridge: James Clarke & Co., 1978), 145.

52. Explained in more detail in *Susie: The Life and Legacy of Susannah Spurgeon*.

53. David Bebbington, *Holiness in Nineteenth-Century England: The 1998 Didsbury Lectures* (Carlisle, Cumbria, UK: Paternoster Press, 2000), 48.

54. Ibid.

55. Ibid.

56. C. H. Spurgeon, *Autobiography*, 4:253.

57. Although Charles resigned from the Union in 1887, his resignation wasn't accepted until 1888.

58. C. H. Spurgeon, *The Cheque Book of the Bank of Faith*, vii.

59. C. H. Spurgeon, *Autobiography*, 4:255.

60. Ibid., 4:254.

61. C. H. Spurgeon, *Autobiography*, 4:256.

62. It is difficult to judge either Spurgeon or his friends as to *how* they waged war in the battle for truth; yet it seems unquestionable that serious theological matters were at stake. Knowing what we do about the character of Charles Spurgeon, he

should receive the benefit of the doubt that he defended the truth in the best ways that he could in his context. The issues of the Down-Grade Controversy needed to be raised and Spurgeon was faithful to wield the sword. Others, who should have been willing to do the same, opted not to rock the denominational boat.

63. Richard Briscoe Cook, *The Wit and Wisdom*, 256.
64. C. H. Spurgeon, *The Cheque Book of the Bank of Faith*, 252.
65. Mrs. C. H. Spurgeon, *Ten Years After!*, 28.
66. Ibid., 28.
67. C. H. Spurgeon, *Autobiography*, 4:348.
68. C. H. Spurgeon, *The Metropolitan Tabernacle Pulpit*, 13:412.

CHAPTER 5: EXPRESSIVE COMMUNICATION

1. *The Morning Post*, London, June 12, 1854, 4.
2. Information in paragraph gathered from various newspaper reports as well as from the British Museum website.
3. C. H. Spurgeon, *Autobiography*, 2:7.
4. Martin Tupper, *Proverbial Philosophy* (Hartford: Solas Andrus & Son, 1854), 100.
5. Iain H. Murray, *Letters of Charles Haddon Spurgeon* (Edinburgh: The Banner of Truth Trust, 1992), 55.
6. C. H. Spurgeon, *Autobiography*, 2:8.
7. Ibid.
8. Iain Murray, *Letters*, 52.
9. C. H. Spurgeon, *Autobiography*, 2:8.
10. Ibid.
11. Ibid., 2:7.
12. Ibid., 2:185.
13. Ibid., 2:185–86.
14. Ibid., 186.
15. Ibid.
16. C. H. Spurgeon, *Spurgeon's Practical Wisdom*, 70.
17. Ibid.
18. Iain Murray, *Letters*, 62.
19. C. H. Spurgeon, *Spurgeon's Practical Wisdom*, 72.
20. C. H. Spurgeon, *An All-Around Ministry: Addresses to Ministers and Students* (London: Passmore and Alabaster, 1900), 250.
21. Charles Spurgeon, (n.d.) "The Letters of C. H. Spurgeon, Collected and Collated by His Son Charles Spurgeon," https://archive.spurgeon.org/misc/letters.php.
22. C. H. Spurgeon, *Lectures to My Students*, 43–44.
23. Iain Murray, *Letters*, 163.
24. Ibid., 164.
25. Ibid., 58.
26. Randolph E. Schmid, (2011) "U.S. Postal Service Survey Reveals Personal Letters at Record Low," *Huffington Post*, http://www.huffingtonpost.com/2011/10/03/postal-service-annual-survey-personal-letters_n_992432.html.

27. Susan Shain, "We Could Use a Little Snail Mail Right Now," *New York Times*, October 8, 2018, https://www.nytimes.com/2018/10/08/smarter-living/we-could-all-use-a-little-snail-mail-right-now.html.
28. C. H. Spurgeon, *Autobiography*, 3:203–4.
29. Ibid., 3:203.
30. Ibid., 204.
31. Ibid., 205.
32. Ibid., 207.
33. Ibid.
34. Ibid., 206.
35. Ibid., 208.
36. Ibid., 209.
37. Ibid., 211.
38. Ibid., 215.
39. Ibid., 216–17.
40. W. Y. Fullerton, *Thomas Spurgeon: A Biography*, 42.
41. C. H. Spurgeon, *Autobiography*, 3:223.
42. Ibid., 230.
43. Ibid., 233.
44. Ibid., 235.
45. Ibid., 237.

CHAPTER 6: LEARNING TOGETHER

1. William Williams, *Personal Reminiscences*, 38.
2. C. H. Spurgeon, *Autobiography*, 4:87.
3. Ibid., 4:89.
4. Iain Murray, *Letters*, 79.
5. Ibid., 12.
6. Ibid.
7. G. Holden Pike, *The Life and Work of Charles Haddon Spurgeon*, 4:378–79.
8. Ibid., 4:327.
9. Ibid., 4:375.
10. C. H. Spurgeon, *Autobiography*, 4:63.
11. Ibid.
12. Ibid., 4:90–91.
13. Ibid., 64–65.
14. Ibid., 68.
15. Ibid., 70.
16. Ibid., 65.
17. C. H. Spurgeon, *Lectures to My Students*, 182.
18. Mrs. C. H. Spurgeon, *A Cluster of Camphire*, 42.
19. C. H. Spurgeon, *Autobiography*, 2:186.
20. C. H. Spurgeon, *Autobiography*, 2:189.

21. C. H. Spurgeon, *The New Park Street Pulpit*, 2:161.
22. C. H. Spurgeon, *Lectures to My Students*, 502.
23. William Williams, *Personal Reminiscences*, 15.
24. Ibid.
25. Mrs. C. H. Spurgeon, *Ten Years After!*, 37.
26. Ibid., 38. This account appears similarly in Ray Rhodes, *Susie: The Life and Legacy of Susannah Spurgeon* (Chicago: Moody Publishers, 2018), 246.
27. Mrs. C.H. Spurgeon, *Ten Years of My Life*, 274.

CHAPTER 7: A TIME TO LAUGH

1. G. Holden Pike, *The Life and Work of Charles Haddon Spurgeon*, 6:308–9.
2. William Williams, *Personal Reminiscences*, 24.
3. C. H. Spurgeon, *An All Around Ministry*, 280–81.
4. C. H. Spurgeon, *The Salt-Cellars: Being a Collection of Proverbs, Together with Homely Notes Thereon* (New York: A.C. Armstrong and Sons, 1889), 1:100.
5. Danzy Sheen, *Pastor C. H. Spurgeon* (London: J. P. Knapp, 1892), 96.
6. Lewis Drummond, *Spurgeon: Prince of Preachers*, 28.
7. C. H. Spurgeon, *According to Promise: Or, The Lord's Method of Dealing with His Chosen People* (New York: Funk and Wagnalls, 1887), 12.
8. Lewis Drummond, *Spurgeon: Prince of Preachers*, 28.
9. Mrs. C. H. Spurgeon, *Ten Years of My Life*, 32.
10. C. H. Spurgeon, *Autobiography*, 3:356.
11. Lewis Drummond, *Spurgeon: Prince of Preachers*, 28.
12. C. H. Spurgeon, *Autobiography*, 3:339.
13. Ibid.
14. Ibid.
15. C. H. Spurgeon, *Lectures to My Students*, 481.
16. C. H. Spurgeon, *Autobiography*, 3:339.
17. Ibid., 3:355.
18. Ibid., 3:340.
19. Ibid.
20. C. H. Spurgeon, *Our Own Hymn Book: A Collection of Psalms and Hymns for Public, Social, and Private Worship* (London: Passmore and Alabaster, 1883), Psalm 100.
21. C. H. Spurgeon, *Autobiography*, 3:346.
22. Ibid., 3:204.
23. Ibid.
24. Ibid.
25. Ibid., 3:207.
26. C. H. Spurgeon, *Autobiography*, 3:347.
27. H. L. Wayland, *Charles H. Spurgeon: His Faith and Works*, 145.
28. C. H. Spurgeon, *Autobiography*, 3:557.
29. C. H. Spurgeon, *Practical Wisdom*, 100.
30. Ibid.
31. Ibid., 101.

32. Ibid., 98.
33. C. H. Spurgeon, *Autobiography*, 3:348.
34. C. H. Spurgeon, *The Metropolitan Tabernacle Pulpit*, 45:174.

CHAPTER 8: HABITS OF A CREATIVE COUPLE

1. William Williams, *Personal Reminiscences*, 19–20.
2. Ibid., 19.
3. Ibid., 21.
4. Ibid., 22.
5. Mark Hopkins, *Nonconformity's Romantic Generation*, 133.
6. The remainder of Spurgeon's library is held at The Midwestern Baptist Theological Seminary, Kansas City, MO. There you can see how varied were Spurgeon's interests.
7. C. H. Spurgeon, *Autobiography*, 3:188.
8. Supplement to *The Bristol Mercury*, September 14, 1861, 2.
9. Ibid.
10. Quoted in Mark Hopkins, *Nonconformity's Romantic Generation*, 129.
11. A. Cunningham Burley, *Spurgeon and His Friendships* (London: The Epworth Press, 1933), 32.
12. Ibid., 34.
13. C. H. Spurgeon, *The Cheque Book of the Bank of Faith*, 10.
14. Ibid.
15. Charles Ray, *The Life and Work of Charles Haddon Spurgeon* (London: Passmore and Alabaster, 1903), 72.
16. Mrs. C. H. Spurgeon, *Ten Years After!*, 12.
17. Ibid.
18. Ibid., 14.
19. William Williams, *Personal Reminiscences*, 33.
20. George Stevenson, *Sketch of the Life and Ministry of the Rev. C. H. Spurgeon* (New York: Sheldon and Company, 1859), 73–74.
21. Charles Haddon Spurgeon, *Spurgeon's Sermons on Family and Home* (Grand Rapids: Kregel, 1995), 136.
22. C. H. Spurgeon, *Autobiography*, 2:175.
23. C. H. Spurgeon, *Eccentric Preachers* (London: Passmore and Alabaster, 1880), 9.
24. Mrs. C. H. Spurgeon, *Ten Years of My Life*, 124.
25. H. I. Wayland, *Charles H. Spurgeon: His Faith and Works*, 227.
26. William Williams, *Personal Reminiscences*, 33.
27. H. L. Wayland, *Charles H. Spurgeon: His Faith and Works*, 234.
28. Ibid.
29. Ibid., 237.
30. C. H. Spurgeon, *Autobiography*, 4:23–24.
31. Ibid., 24–25.
32. Ibid., 4:25.
33. Ibid., 2:187.

34. C. H. Spurgeon, *Autobiography*, 3:184.
35. Ibid., 3:185.
36. Ibid., 3:186–87.
37. Ibid., 3:187.

CHAPTER 9: COMPASSIONATE HEARTS

1. The story of Thomas Johnson is given a very brief treatment in *Susie: The Life and Legacy of Susannah Spurgeon.*
2. Mrs. C. H. Spurgeon, *Ten Years of My Life*, 73–74.
3. Ibid., 74.
4. Ibid., 74–75.
5. Thomas L. Johnson, *Twenty Eight Years a Slave or the Story of My Life in Three Continents* (London: Christian Workers Depot, 1909), iv.
6. Ibid., 1–3.
7. Thomas Johnson, *Twenty-Eight Years*, 32.
8. Ibid.
9. Ibid., 86.
10. Ibid., 90.
11. Ibid., 135.
12. Ibid., 144.
13. Ibid., 212.
14. Ibid., 237.
15. Mike Nicholls, *The Pastor Evangelist*, 56.
16. Ibid., 55.
17. A. Cunningham Burley, *Spurgeon and His Friendships*, 22–23.
18. *Sheffield Weekly Telegraph*, November 2, 1889.
19. Danzy Sheen, *Pastor C. H. Spurgeon*, 99.
20. Larry J. Michael, *Spurgeon on Leadership*, 153.
21. Ibid., 154.
22. C. H. Spurgeon, *Autobiography*, 4:345.
23. A. Cunningham Burley, *Spurgeon and His Friendships*, 26.
24. Charles Ray, *Mrs. C. H. Spurgeon* (1903; repr., Pasadena, TX: Pilgrim Publications, 1973), 48.
25. Mrs. C. H. Spurgeon, *Ten Years of My Life*, 356.
26. Ibid., 357.
27. A. Cunningham Burley, *Spurgeon and His Friendships*, 27.

CHAPTER 10: ETERNAL VISION

1. C. H. Spurgeon, *Autobiography*, 2:27.
2. C. H. Spurgeon, *Autobiography*, 4:337.
3. Ibid., 338.
4. Ibid.
5. Ibid.

6. Ibid.
7. Ibid., 339.
8. Ibid.
9. Ibid.
10. Ibid., 342.
11. Ibid.
12. Ibid.
13. Ibid., 343.
14. Ibid., 345.
15. Ibid.
16. Ibid., 347.
17. Ibid.
18. Ibid., 348–49.
19. Ibid., 350.
20. Ibid., 352.
21. Staff, "7 Reasons Longed for Heaven," The Spurgeon Center, July 13, 2017, https://www.spurgeon.org/resource-library/blog-entries/7-reasons-spurgeon-longed-for-heaven.
22. Quoted in Michael Reeves, *Spurgeon on the Christian Life*, 155.
23. Robert Shindler, *The Life and Labors of Charles Haddon Spurgeon Part II: From the Pulpit to the Palm-Branch* (New York: Gospel Publishing House, n.d.), 16.
24. Ibid.
25. Mrs. C. H. Spurgeon, *Ten Years After!*, 163.
26. Robert Shindler, *From the Pulpit to the Palm-Branch*, 25–26.
27. Ibid., 28.
28. C. H. Spurgeon, *The Sword and the Trowel* (1892), 141.
29. Mrs. C. H. Spurgeon, *Ten Years After!*, 163.
30. Ibid., 163.
31. Robert Shindler, *From the Pulpit to the Palm-Branch*, 23–24.
32. Mrs. C. H. Spurgeon, *Ten Years After!*, v–vi.
33. Robert Shindler, *From the Pulpit to the Palm-Branch*, 27.
34. Ibid., 28.
35. Russell H. Conwell, *Life of Charles H. Spurgeon*, 326–27.
36. Mrs. C. H. Spurgeon, *Ten Years After!*, 164.
37. Robert Shindler, *From the Pulpit to the Palm-Branch*, 29.
38. Ibid.
39. Mrs. C. H. Spurgeon, *Ten Years After!*, vi.
40. Robert Shindler, *From the Pulpit to the Palm-Branch*, 40.
41. Ibid., 40.
42. Mrs. C. H. Spurgeon, *Ten Years After!*, 164.
43. The sermon that Spurgeon revised is no. 2241 in the Metropolitan Tabernacle Pulpit.
44. Robert Shindler, *From the Pulpit to the Palm-Branch*, 38.
45. Ibid.
46. Ernest W. Bacon, *Spurgeon: Heir of the Puritans*, 167.

47. Robert Shindler, *From the Pulpit to the Palm-Branch*, 40–41.
48. Ibid., 43.
49. Ibid.
50. Mrs. C. H. Spurgeon, *Ten Years After!*, 165.
51. Ibid., 164.
52. Ibid., 162.
53. Robert Shindler, *From the Pulpit to the Palm-Branch*, 43–44.
54. Ibid., 50–51.
55. Ibid., 52.
56. Mrs. C. H. Spurgeon, *Ten Years After!*, vi.
57. C. H. Spurgeon, *Autobiography*, 1:127.
58. C. H. Spurgeon, *The Sword and the Trowel* (1892), 141–42.
59. Ibid., 140.
60. C. H. Spurgeon, *Autobiography*, 2:2.
61. C. H. Spurgeon, *The Sword and the Trowel* (1892), 109.
62. Charles Ray, *Mrs. C. H. Spurgeon*, 116.

EPILOGUE: YOURS, TILL HEAVEN, *AND THEN*

1. The tablet was installed April 1897; therefore, Thomas's visit was sometime afterwards.
2. W. Y. Fullerton, *Thomas Spurgeon: A Biography*, 3.
3. Ibid.
4. C. H. Spurgeon, *Practical Wisdom*, 100.
5. Charles Spurgeon, "Christ's Love to His Spouse," https://www.spurgeon.org/resource-library/sermons/christs-love-to-his-spouse/#flipbook.
6. E. L. Magoon, *The Modern Whitefield: The Rev. C. H. Spurgeon of London, His Sermons* (New York: Sheldon. Blakeman. and Company, 1856), 299.
7. C. H. Spurgeon, Spurgeon's Sermons, "Morning and Evening 7/22 AM," OnePlace.com, https://www.oneplace.com/ministries/spurgeon-sermons/read/devotionals/spurgeons-morning-and-evening/morning-and-evening-722-am-551238.html.
8. Mrs. C. H. Spurgeon, *Ten Years After!*, 170.
9. Charles Ray, *Mrs. C. H. Spurgeon*, 112.
10. C. H. Spurgeon, *The Sword and the Trowel* (1865), 460.

Church where Spurgeon was converted in 1850. It was then a Primitive Methodist congregation. Photo courtesy of Ray Rhodes Jr.

Site of Spurgeon's baptism on May 3, 1850, in the River Lark at Isleham. Photo courtesy of Ray Rhodes Jr.

Tablet of Spurgeon's conversion at the Artillery Street Church in Colchester, placed in 1897. Photo courtesy of Ray Rhodes Jr.

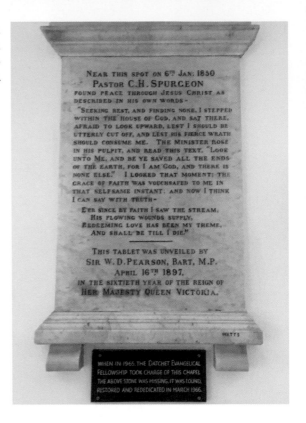

This photo is from a postcard commemorating the grand opening of the Crystal Palace in 1854. By permission of Crystal Palace Foundation.

Queen Victoria opening the Crystal Palace on June 10, 1854, at Sydenham. This is the night and the place where Charles first revealed his romantic interest in Susie.

Crystal Fountain at the Crystal Palace where Charles and Susie met weekly during their engagement from August 1854–December 1855. By permission of Crystal Palace Foundation.

Photo of Charles and Susie's marriage certificate. Courtesy of Pastor T. D. Hale.

Hotel Le Meurice in Paris (as it looks today), where Charles and Susie stayed during their honeymoon in January 1856. Hotel is in the same location though the building has been completely redone. Then, as now, it was considered to be one of the greatest hotels in the world. Photo courtesy of Ray Rhodes Jr.

Notre Dame Cathedral, Paris. Charles and Susie visited most of the notable Paris cathedrals during their honeymoon in January 1856. Susie was at Notre Dame earlier on the eve of Napoleon III's wedding to Eugénie in January 1853. Photo courtesy of Ray Rhodes Jr.

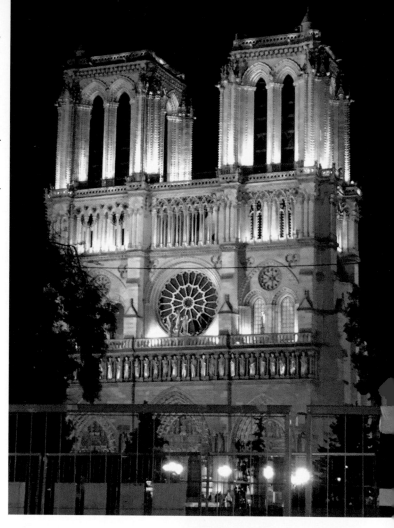

Charles and Susie in their home at Nightingale Lane, c. 1867 - c. 1869. Courtesy of Pastor T. D. Hale.

Charles and Susie at their second home, "Helensburgh House" on Nightingale Lane, circa 1857–58. Courtesy of Pastor T. D. Hale.

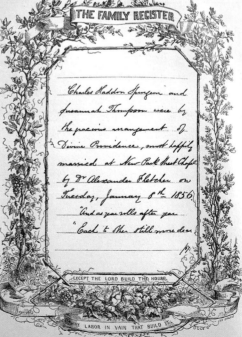

THE FAMILY REGISTER

Charles Haddon Spurgeon and Susannah Thompson were by the precious arrangement of Divine Providence, most happily married at New Park Street Chapel by Dr Alexander Fletcher on Tuesday, January 8th 1856. "And as years rolls after year "Each to other still more dear

EXCEPT THE LORD BUILD THE HOUSE.

THEY LABOR IN VAIN THAT BUILD IT.

Marriage registry in Charles and Susie's family Bible. Taken from *C. H. Spurgeon's Autobiography.*

Charles and Susie at their home on Nightingale Lane. Circa 1857–59. Courtesy of Pastor T. D. Hale.

Interior of Sainte-Chapelle, Paris, one of the cathedrals that Charles and Susie visited on their honeymoon. Charles referred to it as "a little heaven of stained glass." Photo courtesy of Ray Rhodes Jr.

Charles and Susie's first home together in January 1856, 217 New Kent Road, London. Photo from *C. H. Spurgeon's Autobiography*.

Charles and Susie's second home, "The Helensburgh House" on Nightingale Lane. They lived here from late 1857–68. Photo taken from *C. H. Spurgeon's Autobiography*.

Charles and Susie's third home, the second Helensburgh House on Nightingale Lane. This house was built on the site of their second home. They moved into this home in 1869 and left in 1880. Photo from *C. H. Spurgeon's Autobiography*.

Westwood: Last home of Charles and Susie. They moved here in 1880. Charles died in 1892 and Susie in 1903. The home was eventually sold. The house no longer stands and the property is the site of a school. Photo from Charles Ray's book *The Life of Charles Haddon Spurgeon*.

The Pastors' College was started in 1856. This building was constructed in 1874. Charles and Susie invested a significant amount from their own funds to support the college. Susie was called "The Mother of the College." Courtesy of Pastor T. D. Hale.

Front of Spurgeon's Metropolitan Tabernacle as it is today. The Tabernacle opened in 1861. The front is essentially unchanged from Spurgeon's day. Photo courtesy of Ray Rhodes Jr.

Susie with twin sons, Charles and Thomas, around 1866. The twins were 10 years old and Susie was 32. Courtesy of Pastor T. D. Hale.

Susie (date unknown). Courtesy of Pastor T. D. Hale.

Susie seated outside
(date unknown).
Courtesy of Pastor T. D. Hale.

Susie seated (date unknown).
Courtesy of Pastor T. D. Hale.

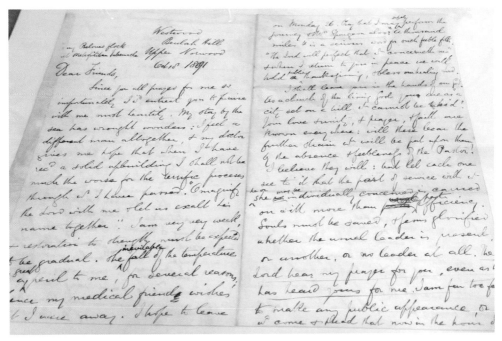

This letter is from Charles to his congregation just prior to when he left with Susie on his last trip to Mentone, October 1891. The trip was the first time that Susie had been with him to Mentone. Charles died in Mentone in January 1892. Photo taken by Ray Rhodes Jr. Used by permission from the Metropolitan Tabernacle.

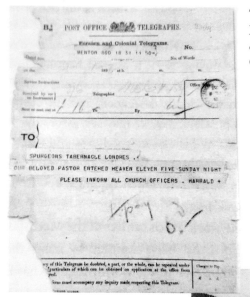

Telegram from Mentone to the Metropolitan Tabernacle, telling of Charles Spurgeon's death. Courtesy of Pastor T. D. Hale.

Hotel Beau-Rivage, Mentone, where Charles Spurgeon died. Courtesy of Pastor T. D. Hale.

Charles Spurgeon's coffin. Courtesy of Pastor T. D. Hale.